BUSINESS
GPS

Finding Your Way Through the
Worst Time of Your Life

JOSEPH MEUSE

ISBN: 979-8-9857-901-0-8

Publisher: Tolle Lege Press, a division of Bravera Holdings, LLC
Editor: Liz Martin
Designer: Ricacabrex (fiverr.com)
Proofing: Lita Sanders & Jan Vallorani

CONTENTS

PREFACE

R ealization hit the pit of my stomach.

I had started in 2008, after 19 years of running businesses. It felt like I'd just lost the last balloon from the bunch that were holding my house in the air. The whole thing was about to crash on the edge of a cliff, and I wasn't sure how I would keep it from falling over the edge completely.

That feeling started to grow into desperation.

I had just gotten off the phone with the nastiest guy I had dealt with to date — and he was promising to sue me.

Who could blame him? Why wouldn't he? My business was scraping the bottom of the cash barrel and coming up short. I literally didn't have the funds to pay my obligations. I had nowhere to turn. There was no money to be had.

Have you ever heard the old expression, "didn't have two nickels to rub together" and thought something along the lines of "that poor bastard?"

This was me now, only I didn't even have even the one nickel to call heads or tails. And it sure felt like it had been tails for a while.

It wasn't because my business hadn't done well: it had been sailing along brilliantly! I had started in 2008, after 33 years of running businesses. In fact, I had started my first company at 19! It helped to pay my way through William & Mary. It's always come naturally to me, the art and science of starting businesses. The entrepreneurial bug bit me young and kept on biting.

While not every business I'd started was a resounding success — my first business actually got edged out of the market by quality controls that I didn't have control over — this one had been doing well...I thought.

2008 was a rough year in many industries, and mine was hit the hardest. 2009 and 2010 were the leanest years I had faced in over 30, and I wasn't sure I was going to make it. I would call my CPA weekly to figure out where I was, what I could do, and how long we could last.

His solution was like many offered by those in the finance world: cut your expenses and increase your revenue. Well, yeah...of course! But how?

In a downturn, when everyone in the industry is feeling the belt tightening around their necks and not just their waists, how do you just "find more revenue?" How do you "cut expenses" when you're literally operating on bare bones already?

His response was to turn my retainer from monthly invoicing into a pre-paid account.

My next call was to my attorney. "They're suing me. I can't afford to pay anything. What do I do?" He says he'll call them and a few days later, he came back to me.

"Great news, Joe! I got your debt settled! All you have to do is pay $10,000 a month for 10 months and when you've paid that $100,000, your full debt will be charged off!"

I don't think he had understood my first statement to him: I can't afford to pay *anything*.

Like my CPA, his response was to turn my account from a retainer at monthly invoicing into pre-paid only.

This situation taught me this more than anything: you have to think outside the box.

Let's face it, CPAs and attorneys are truly taught to think inside the proverbial box: regulations, rules, penalties, laws, ethics. There's not a lot of leeway for creativity outside of the fictional show Just Call Saul for attorneys and CPAs.

And this is where we find the loophole. You can legally and ethically develop a plan outside of the box and create a situation that works for you.

I remembered. There was a guy I had run into a few times. He called himself a debt negotiator. "What would you do in this situation," I asked him. "How do I resolve my debts without paying money I don't have?"

Most lawyers advise to show no weakness. Come in strong, make promises to do everything. CPAs spend their days trying to work your numbers into their best shape to show maximum profitability and excess lendability. Both create a Savior dynamic: they're the experts and can save you from the situation. But in the end, you'll find their inside-the-box results aren't going to benefit *you*.

You have to think around the corners and determine the creative escape that is legal, ethical, and beneficial to *you*.

The debt negotiator's approach was somewhat humbling. He shared my actual financials with my lenders. I wasn't fooling when I said I literally didn't have two nickels to rub together, and there was literally no way to squeeze the money from this stone. They saw that. They were going to get nothing or nothing unless they worked with my negotiator on a creative solution.

In this type of situation, most will believe they have no control over the outcome and that belief turns into fear. How will I support my family? How will I take care of my employees? What will people say about my business if it fails? How will I live?

Fear keeps you inside the box. Fear keeps you out of control. Fear causes you to lose the swagger that attracts business to what you do best.

How do you conquer the fear and regain control over your situation when it feels like everything is lost?

That's what I'm going to talk about in the next few pages. Because when I went looking for answers and guidance, I could find a book on every business topic except how to get out of the hole and get back on top again. I was alone in a sea of advice on every other topic but this one: how do I legally, ethically, and creatively get through this?

And that debt negotiator who showed my underbelly to the overlords? They settled for a total of $18,000 over 3 months. That's a lot better than $100,000 over 10 months.

Since then, I have helped over 2,000 business owners in similarly dire (or even worse) situations work their way out of the worst days of their lives and back into the best.

I've helped them achieve financial freedom: the key to what makes life, liberty, and the pursuit of what makes you happy possible. I've not just helped them get back on their feet, I've watched them excel to the great heights of strong business once again.

This is my goal for you, too. If you're reading this book and find my personal story resonating, you know that I know how you feel right now. And I know that I can help you, too. Let's get started!

-Joe

PART 1

HOW DID I GET HERE?

CHAPTER ONE

COMMON PROBLEMS THAT DESTROY BUSINESSES AND CASTRATE ENTREPRENEURS

O ver 2,000 businesses that I have worked with over the past decade have many differences. Different industries, people, financials, challenges. Their KPIs and SOPs are varied, and no two mission statements are alike.

There are many factors that play into a business achieving success or suffering failure. Quality controls, competition, economy, hiring decisions.

Perhaps it was a restaurateur who built in the wrong neighborhood and found food waste destroying his margins. Perhaps it was a contractor who found himself on the southern end of a collapsing housing market.

Any business owner could find himself edged out by his competitors, facing personal challenges that overwhelm his mind and deplete his bank account.

Every business has a game plan, a set of plays that work. Setting the right prices, creating the right benefits to attract the right team, putting customer service first, offering a specific commodity that no one else can. This is what makes you great at what you do.

But there are a few things that will take your business off track. It might be quickly, but more likely it will be in such small increments that you likely will not even notice it happening. You wake up one day and say, "what the hell happened!"

But the truth is, it's probably been happening for a while. You're just now noticing. Why?

While many business owners share the same goal as most of us (to make money and enjoy doing it), there have been three similarities that I have found in a business that has an owner finding themself spiraling into a drain of desperation, fear, and lack of control.

- Financial ignorance
- Excess of Ego
- Denial

Ouch! That hurt, I know.

Before I lose you, let me remind you that I've been here, too. I've stared down that drain and felt the swirl of loss all around me.

Loss of my financial security; loss of my home; loss of the respect of my peers, employees, perhaps even a partner or spouse.

There are a lot of painful moments while you're spiraling down that drain.

It's a lot less painful to look in the mirror and figure out where you can adjust to slow or even stop that downward trend.

50% of businesses fail to make it through their fifth year. Why is that? And how do you avoid being one of them…or worse, one of the 30% that fail after being successful for over a decade?

Let's talk about these three things that can cause a business to fail.

FINANCIAL IGNORANCE

First: financial ignorance because this is absolutely the most important. I'm not suggesting that every business owner has to be a CPA, or have an MBA. The goal is for you to understand your business's specific financials.

What are the key metrics?

What defines a good day or a bad day?

What makes your business operate for another week versus shutting down?

What keeps the lights on and what keeps everyone receiving fat bonus checks at the end of the year?

Likely you're the only person who can truly answer what your ultimate goals are for your business. Is it to make a living until retirement? Is it to make it big so that you can retire early? Is it to achieve great things so that your finances can go where your passions lie? Is it to 3x your current revenue? 10x?

Regardless of your goals, you are the one who has the vision and you have to guide the business towards those goals. Your employees cannot do that for you; the best employees are still working for you, for your business, for your goals. So you have to know what is going to get you there, and what you and your team have to do to get there. And you must communicate it to them.

Especially to the people who have their fingers on the pulse of your business 24/7: your accounting personnel.

In some cases, this is going to mean you sit down more often than you might like to look at the numbers: the nitty-gritty details of where your pennies went, and it's likely going to chafe against your nature.

You're going to have to have more conversations with your accounting team than anyone truly wants to have with their accounting team. And sometimes they're going to be difficult and painful conversations.

But you've got to eliminate whatever it is that is keeping you from fully understanding your business's financials week-to-week, day-to-day, hour-to-hour.

We'll be talking about this in-depth as we go along. Know your business's financial status. Feel its pulse hourly if necessary. Communicate to your bookkeepers and they will have a better understanding of what to alert you to, what to warn you about, what to raise a red flag over.

EXCESS OF EGO

Ego is not in and of itself a bad thing. The Latin translation of ego is literally "I." It's what makes yourself you. The more common vernacular as popularized by Freud is the "complex of ego," the excess of ego. And this is where we confer.

The excess of ego looks in the mirror and thinks, "I don't need help; I can figure this out on my own." It pushes against the spiral with one hand and waves its other hand. I've gotten out of this kind of scrape before. I can do it again. No one needs to know how close we are to failing.

Excess of ego keeps us from understanding where we really are, where we are headed if we don't make some possibly radical changes and will eventually land us in a septic tank of you know what with little hope of exit.

Excess of ego will destroy — has destroyed — countless businesses and business owners, their families, and affected countless employees and their families.

To bolster our fragile egos, we credit our successes to our own brilliance and skill, and we attribute our failures to the shortcomings of others or to events outside our control. This pattern is so deeply ingrained that psychologists have labeled it the Fundamental Attribution Error.

As an example of the behavior which attribution error theory seeks to explain, consider the situation where a driver named Bob is cut off in traffic by Cathy.

Bob attributes Cathy's behavior to her fundamental personality, e.g., she thinks only of herself, she is selfish, she is a jerk, she is an unskilled driver. He does not think it is perhaps situational, e.g., she is going to miss her flight, her daughter is convulsing at school, or her mother was just rushed to the hospital with a heart attack.

Bob might well make another mistake and excuse his outrage at Cathy by saying he was influenced by situational causes, e.g., I am late for my job interview, I must pick up my son for his dental appointment, rather than thinking he has a character flaw, e.g., I am such a jerk, I treat others with contempt, I am bad at driving.[1]

When we hold onto an excess of ego, we tend to blame others (employees, situations, customers, vendors, the economy) instead of looking at where we might have had a problem, and we tend to over-inflate our own sense of worth, value, acumen, skill. We tend to under-accept where our failings might have occurred.

The great Roman emperor and philosopher-extraordinaire Marcus Aurelius would point out that every day you will

---

1   Paraphrased from *Ethics Unwrapped*. McCombs School of Business, The University of Texas at Austin. 2018

encounter "interference, ingratitude, insolence, disloyalty, ill-will, and selfishness — all of them due to the offenders' ignorance." But he goes on to point out: "None of those things can injure me, for nobody can implicate me in what is degrading. Neither can I be angry with my brother or fall foul of him; for he and I were born to work together, like a man's two hands, feet or eyelids, or the upper and lower rows of his teeth. To obstruct each other is against Nature's law — and what is irritation or aversion but a form of obstruction."[2]

John Rampton is an entrepreneur, investor and startup enthusiast, and the founder of the calendar productivity tool Calendar. He wrote a 2016 *Entrepreneur* article, "8 Ways My Ego Killed My Business".

It starts like this: "Years ago I had a successful startup that I sold for a lot of money. I thought because I did this that I could do anything. I let my ego run my life. I started a new venture and acted like I was "the bomb" and nothing could stop me. This destroyed my business. It wasn't the company, product, or people behind the business... it was 100% me that killed this company. As a result, I lost almost everything I owned."

Author Ryan Holiday records more than a few examples of an excess of ego destroying successful — even iconic — brands in his book *Ego Is the Enemy*. Excess of ego has been the downfall of nations and many powerful regimes. We could point out Xerxes the Persian, who, when the river dared to destroy bridges he had just built, literally sent men to whip the river with chains and burn

---

2   Marcus Aurelius, *Meditations* 2.1.

it with hot irons. The heads of the men who built the bridges were also separated from their bodies, for who would dare to let the great emperor down?

Another story says Xerxes wrote a letter to a mountain he was tunneling through, demanding it bow to his will or he would "topple it into the sea." Such preposterous outcries, such "presumptuous displays," as the historian Herodotus would call Xerxes excess of ego.

Creator of Beanie Babies, Ty Warner, narrowly escaped jail just ahead of his business's implosion despite his egotistical boast that he could "put the Ty heart on manure and they'd buy it."

Listen to the infamous Oval Office tapes of Richard Nixon and you'll hear a man whose excess of ego has overtaken his sense of right, wrong, duty, honor, and what his role as the Commander in Chief for the people of the United States of America was supposed to be.

Perhaps the most succinct warning of how an excess of ego exhibits itself is that of a critic of Napoleon Bonaparte: "He despises the nation whose applause he seeks." Of course, that very nation sent one of the most prolific conquerors the world would ever know into exile, and wreaked havoc on his rule.

Modern historians would debate whether he was an enlightened but perhaps misguided ruler who would lay the foundations of modern civilization across Europe, or a tyrannical megalomaniac who wrought more misery than anyone prior to Hitler.

But the tyrannical megalomania recognized in Napoleon's actions as detailed in our history books is not always so easy to spot.

Legend Harold Geneen, the CEO of ITT who is largely recognized as a pioneer in mergers and acquisitions that launched the world of international conglomerates, compared an excess of ego to alcoholism: "The egotist does not stumble about, knocking things off his desk. He does not stammer or drool. No, instead he becomes more and more arrogant, and some people, not knowing what is underneath such an attitude, mistake his arrogance for a sense of power and self-confidence." It's not always easy to recognize, particularly in oneself.

In the era of bar carts in the office and a steady stream of secretaries delivering ice for the clinking glasses of Senior Partner and Junior Account Manager alike, as shown in the hit AMC show *Mad Men*, alcoholism was the popular perpetrator of a businessman's doom. But Geneen disagreed it was the worst enemy, and so do I. He left no doubt of his opinion in his memoirs:

"Whether in middle management or top management, unbridled personal egotism blinds a man to the realities around him; more and more he comes to live in a world of his own imagination; and because he sincerely believes he can do no wrong, he becomes a menace to the men and women who have to work under his direction."

American Entrepreneur and investor Adeo Ressi's Founder Institute studied over 15,000 aspiring entrepreneurs and concluded that the attributes of "Bad Founder DNA" are: excuse-making, predatory aggressiveness, deceit, emotional instability, and narcissism.

All of these traits are habits, habits developed by an excess of ego and fed by an excess of ego. Ego that can — and will likely — destroy your business. Ego that will destroy your relationships, and quite possibly the quality of your life. Excess of Ego is one of the worst enemies of a successful endeavor, because it will constantly present a stone to trip over, a boulder in the way of laying your tracks, a mountain to climb over.

An excess of ego won't listen to advice, despite it being painfully clear that the situation they're in is providing evidence that they may need to listen to someone else's advice because what they're doing isn't working. "It is impossible to learn that which one thinks one already knows," a warning given to us by Epictetus. But as an old proverb says, "When a student is ready, the teacher appears."

When financial ignorance is paired with an excess of ego, you will almost certainly find a cemetery of businesses that failed to succeed, many even well beyond the expectation of failure phase, that first five-year start-up period.

The skill of accepting advice, even perhaps critical feedback, and being told your situation needs someone else's skillset may hurt, but it is absolutely imperative you swallow your ego and listen.

Because an excess of ego often means we find ourselves looking in the mirror and seeing nothing wrong, which leads us to the third commonality in businesses that find themselves struggling.

DENIAL

We're probably all familiar with the Kubler-Ross model — commonly known as the Five Stages of Grief.

Swiss-American psychologist Elisabeth Kubler-Ross found in her work with terminally ill patients that most people, when faced with such life-altering news, experience times of denial, bargaining, anger, depression, and finally, acceptance.

While Kubler-Ross noted later in life, like many of us who have experienced grief at its rawest form, these expressions of grief are not a linear progression. They are not complete at the end, nor are they necessarily in "that order," nor do they necessarily magically dissipate once one has experienced all 5. And in her posthumously published work with David Kessler, a sixth "stage" was added: that of meaning.

Kübler-Ross also expanded her model from terminal illness to include any form of personal loss, such as the death of a loved one, the loss of a job or income, major rejection, the end of a relationship or divorce, drug addiction, incarceration, the onset of a disease or an infertility diagnosis, and even minor losses like that of a promotion.

Perhaps it is in the rejection of what you know to be a great offer, or an employee who exits the company to pursue another line of work — or worse, a competitor.

Anyone who has lost a business knows that grief is definitely a strong effect of such a loss and has likely been expressed in the full gamut of Kubler-Ross stages.

Which brings us around to that first stage: denial.

What does denial look like in a business environment? It's when your accountant says, "Hey, there's something you might need to see," and you brush it off and head to your office to make sales calls.

It's when you feel like there's something wrong, but you push the feeling aside to go to dinner and the movies.

It's when you get that call from the lender who hasn't been paid in 6 months and you try to say things aren't as bad as they seem.

It's when your sales have been declining for months but you insist it's just temporary and the saving grace is on the horizon, without any adjustment or shift of your business model, operations, practices, or thought processes.

Denial will cost you because it is a lack of control. And when you're spiraling down the drain, you need to be in control, not denying the situation as it is at this moment.

Facts are better than dreams, said Churchill. John D. Rockefeller would tell himself, "Keep your eyes open. Don't lose your balance." No one likes to be in a bad situation, but it is far worse to embrace denial instead of reality.

Take a deep breath. Look in the mirror. Say goodbye to the excess of ego, put an end to the denial, and put into motion the effort to truly understand your business's financials. If you're willing to do these three things, you've just put yourself ahead of many others who lie in that business graveyard.

Let's dig deep and figure out how you got here so we can get you out.

CHAPTER TWO

OVERNIGHT VS. OVER TIME

You've put on a few pounds since college. Your metabolism has slowed down, and you watch what you eat a little less in the stress of business start-up and maintenance than you did when you were a starter on the varsity football team. A few sessions at the gym each week has turned into a New Year's Resolution that fizzles before February.

After a few years of burgers and beer, that few extra has turned into a full 250+ pounds of excess weight and your doctor's given you a warning about the health of your heart, knees, and a list of pills you're about to have to take if you don't get back to working out and lose that extra weight.

So you sign up for the gym, and the first day you walk in to talk to the trainer. "I want to lose this extra 250 pounds in the next two hours."

Crazy, right? We all know that you not only can't, but you shouldn't lose weight that quickly! The fitness trainer is going to say, "It's going to take some time to work it off."

After all, you didn't put it on in a few hours, so you aren't going to get it off in a few hours either. You can't skip ahead to Z if you're not willing to start with ABC.

Your business woes are the same as those extra pounds. While there could be that "one thing" that might put your business over the cliff, like a client backing out of a year-making deal, or a vital vendor unable to supply at the necessary price, generally speaking it is slow, incremental erosion that puts your business into a downward spiral, not one single event. And now it's going to take some time to get out of that spiral.

This is one reason I so strongly urge financial understanding. When you've prioritized understanding the specific financial necessities your business requires to be successful, when your finger is on the pulse of what makes your business make it another day or warns you that you might be heading for trouble, you're able to catch — and halt — that erosion.

But I'm busy, you'll say. I have so much to do, and that's what Susie in accounting was hired to do! How many times have I heard a business owner put the onus of the financial health of his business on a hired hand.

That isn't to say Susie isn't an exceptional accountant. She may be an exceptional employee overall. But she is not *you*. She is not ever going to be *you*.

There's no doubt you are sun-up to sun-down busy. Every business owner has too much to do, that's no lie. And you may be more skilled in other areas or enjoy them more.

I'm on the front lines with nearly 500 businesses at a time. Nearly every business owner I have worked with has underestimated the amount of financial understanding of their business from day to day that they must have in order for their business to make it another month.

Developing a financial health muscle is much like any other muscle. Work it out, and eventually you will find it easier to work it out. No one else on your team is going to quite work it out to the level that you will. They'll follow your lead.

So train every day. Work out every day. You're headed for a marathon, and you need to be prepared for it. You cannot rely on someone else to work out for you, and likewise you cannot expect the financial health of your business to rely on someone else.

It doesn't matter what business you're in: you cannot make the assumption that your accounting person or team is going to keep your business on track financially. That's always going to come down to you, the business owner, and how well they do at keeping your business on track will rely on your level of communication with them.

Knowing your business's financial health must be your number one priority. Communicating with your accounting person/team is number two. The more you do it, the easier it will become to understand what is going on in your business, what is working, what is not working. What helps, what hurts. You have to live and breathe your financials.

Perhaps there have been other papercuts that have sliced your business health. Having the wrong people on your team can be as detrimental as not having the right people on your team.

In his book *Entreleadership*, financial guru Dave Ramsey includes in his "Five Enemies of a Unified Team" three important personnel issues: gossip, unresolved disagreements, sanctioned incompetence. Jim Collins reiterates the importance of good hiring in his must-read bestseller *Good to Great*.

Where does the ultimate responsibility lie? Leadership, of course. That's you. It means being the right kind of leader, not only one who is financially aware and also does not indulge in excess of ego, but it also means one more thing: the ability to make decisions that could be very hard to make. Ones that could mean letting someone go because they haven't been the right person in the right seat in your company and could ultimately harm your business if they stay.

Because the second most important responsibility is having the right people on your team. Over time, having the wrong people in the seats can severely damage your business and possibly destroy it.

Or perhaps you found yourself humming along, great employees running your successful business and for once, you've relaxed a little. You've slowed down, perhaps you're not spending as many hours at the office as you are on the golf course. After all, you've earned it! You've worked very hard to garner this success, you might as well enjoy some of the rewards.

Taking your hands off the reins may have allowed you some extra time with family, friends, and fun, and that is no crime. But there is truth in the statement I made previously: you are the one who will care the most about your business. If you're not there in it day-to-day, will it not only survive but thrive without you?

If you've let go of ownership or passed off so much responsibility to your team that you're not exactly sure what's going on, you've taken your finger off the pulse, and you may have no idea if your business is actually healthy... or going to make it out alive.

When your hands are off the reins, when complacency has set in, and an ignorance of your financial health has overtaken you, this is when your business will flounder. You'll find yourself called by a trained and hostile collection agency, and you'll have no idea what you can and cannot do to get out of this mess.

You may be facing judgements that will affect your freedom, the opinions of others about you, even the survival of your life as you know it.

The biggest risks to your business are the risks you could see coming but don't pay attention to until they slap you in the face.

It didn't take a minute or a day to get where you are now, and it won't take a minute or a day to get you out of it. You're going to have to trust the process will take some time and work out day by day until you're strong and healthy again.

But I'm here to offer you not only hope, but proof that it is possible!

CHAPTER THREE

THE IMPORTANCE OF TIME

When people come to me, they're often at the end of their rope. Time has run out for them, or so they believe. They've usually tried everything else: banks, merchant cash advances, even family loans.

Many entrepreneurs have put their savings and possibly even their homes on the line for their business. Often, you'll see loans stacked on other loans, lines of credit taken against life insurance policies.

And buried in the midst of all this, you'll find a desperate entrepreneur who has a family, employees and their families, vendors and their families, hundreds of humans depending on the company's survival for their own. It's a heavy burden to bear! And it's all at risk of crashing down around them... or perhaps it's already started crashing.

At the apparent end of the rope, they somehow find me. Perhaps by word of mouth or by a Google search, and they've reached out for a consultation. I charge a flat fee to start, but if someone says to me, "I don't even have that," I've lowered it to what they can pay.

Why?

Because I'm not in the business of greed, I'm in the business of offering a lifeline to a drowning business owner who has a business worth saving.

How do I know if a business is worth it? If the owner is willing to listen to my advice.

Let's talk about that excess of ego once more: 90% of the potential clients I have turned down has been because they're not willing to listen to my advice. Time is an asset, and I am not going to waste my time — and theirs — convincing them to follow the advice they asked me to give to them.

When you're at the end of your rope, and you believe you've run out of time, there is no time to waste.

Concurrently, every week you're able to hang on, every day you're able to get through, that is putting you one step closer to yet another week you'll hang on to, another day you'll get through.

Every day or week that we're able to get you through is another day and week your business has to make money and turn a corner. I'll help you figure out what you need to do now. Today.

And then tomorrow.

And the next day.

And next week.

We will talk more later on about the golden asset of time, and about long-term plans, but for now, when you're at the bottom of your rope and you believe you have no more time, time is what I will get for you.

Time is what you need most, and time is what you'll be able to get.

CHAPTER FOUR

WHAT IT'S GOING TO TAKE TO GET OUT

Right about now you're probably asking, so how *do* I get out of this mess? How can I not only dig out of this hole, but also come back to crest the mountain once more?

- Trust the advice.
- Balance humility with swagger.
- Learn from it all.

There are no code-cracking skills involved in the process of getting out of the worst time of your life. You didn't get here with the wave of a wand, and you won't get out by it either. It's going to take time — and trust.

You are going to have to balance between being the most humble you've ever had to be, and regaining your confidence so that you swagger once again. And in order to rebuild back even better, you're going to need to learn from it all. Without learning from it, you are likely doomed to repeat it.

You're not going to get back on top by making a slight adjustment. This is not a ten-degree shift to come out on top. We're talking about ninety-degree shifts. Drastic measures that may be uncomfortable up front but will save you — and your business — to fight another day.

But first let's talk about trusting the advice. As I mentioned before, 90% of the potential clients I turn down have an excess of ego and refuse to trust my advice. They know better. They inevitably will waste their time, and mine.

I'm not desperate, and if they won't listen to my expertise on how to get out of the downward spiral they're launching into, apparently neither are they. I move on. I'm unwilling to accept money for my time. I need results, victories with my clients. If they cannot listen, accept, and achieve the results I know I can provide, I have to move on.

But for the guy who says, "help," it doesn't matter how quietly or how long it takes for him to say it, or if he can pay me $100 when he says it, when he says "help me," and means it, I'm there.

Maybe he can't afford my initial fee requirement. Is he willing to follow my advice? Then I'll work with him. Because there is nearly no business that cannot be saved and no business owner who can't be helped if they follow my advice.

That's not to say that I am responsible for the fix of a dastardly downward spiral. It takes partnership. You are the key figure in this scenario. I'm more like your Spirit Guide, helping you, encouraging you, telling you what will help this particular situation. But you must not accept defeat and let another General take the glory. This will be on you to work through, get through, and dig out until you're back on top again.

For example, the owner of a pharmaceutical company located in Southern California faced seemingly insurmountable odds personally and professionally.

At the same time his business was expanding from a 5,000 square foot facility into a 66,000 square foot facility, a big jump, and a huge stressor in any business owner's life, he lost his young wife to cancer and found out his oldest child, only 7 years old, had contracted leukemia. He walked away from his operating business.

He was a broken man, and unashamedly so. He was facing the worst possible outcomes including life without his spouse, facing the most woeful crisis with his child that any parent can realize, 2 IRS audits, 24 judgements, and a foreclosure notice.

This was an extremely tough situation — for both of us. Not only did we need to repair the business, we had to work to repair the man himself.

Thankfully we had some initial victories that created trust. He was very stressed and nervous, a beaten down person who had experienced all the worst of the worst. Swagger? None. Hope?

None. Keeping calm with him helped to get his decision-making back on track so that he could dig out of the mire.

I started to visit with him once a month, then twice a month, each time our relationship building better and better, and he took more of my advice. The key was rebuilding his confidence so that he made the right decisions. We spent time together personally, too, talking about life and how the business served his life goals and purpose.

The 2 IRS audits (with over $6 million in exposure) were closed at zero cost. We were able to turn those 24 judgments against him into term loans and he paid approximately 50 cents on the dollar over 4 years, saving him around $3 million.

We were able to buy enough time with the bank who held the mortgage on his house to capitalize on the Covid real estate boom. He did not make a mortgage payment for almost 2 years, but with the time we bought him, and a global crisis created by an unforeseen situation allowed his building to be sold for $23 million, with a lease back option — netting this owner $9 million dollars and the opportunity to keep his business operating.

Time is your biggest asset. Figure out how to maintain your swagger. Learn from past mistakes. Drop the ego and trust my advice, and the results will deliver.

You might be saying, but Joe, I trusted Susie in accounting, and she didn't warn me. I trusted these lenders to have my back. I trusted my family to be behind me. Look where it's led me!

I'll say it again: I have been where you are right now. I can feel what you're feeling. I won't leave you hanging, and you can trust that my expertise in this area can help you, too. In the dark of night when you're feeling the fear closing you into that box, when you're in the middle of a hellacious day and the collector's just reamed you, you can email me, text me, get me on the phone. We'll inch back the control into your hands. Trust the process.

Let's talk about control. When you're in the death grip of spiraling into the worst moments of your life, the natural inclination is to believe you're not in control. You're likely facing angry lenders, trained vultures who are hell-bent on separating you from your money or your sanity…or both.

You may be facing the rage of a partner, spouse, family member, or trusted friend whose opinion matters, even perhaps more than you'd like to admit. You're probably also fearful of the end result of "the end of the world as you know it." No one wants to struggle, and when you're facing the position you've found yourself in, you're struggling to check out of the McDonald's drive-thru when you're very used to enjoying Tomahawk Ribeyes, $450 bottles of wine, and tuna tartare at the best places in town.

Not to mention, it's your baby on the line here! It's likely your life savings, your sweat equity, your blood and tears and a lot of sweat that have been poured into employees who count on you, clients and customers who will be disappointed, vendors who will be angry and upset to remain unpaid.

You're possibly staring in the mirror wondering where you've gone wrong, what have you done, what can you do to fix this. The questions, even possibly the guilt that is ravaging your mind, seem insurmountable.

You've lost the confidence you had, that swagger that you had getting into the elevator and punching the button for your floor. That swagger is your pride in doing a good job, having a team following your lead, and customers who love you. It's vendors who send you big gift baskets at the end of the year, and the wins that you have accumulated over the years you've been doing business that adorn your walls.

Now, you're feeling the void. The loss of confidence is because you're actually failing, probably in the biggest way you never imagined possible.

Don't get me wrong, this is a tough time and you're not an idiot for feeling the humility of horrible conversations and the worst moments of your life. But you've got to get your swagger back. You're going to have to dig deep.

Fight for it. Fight for the shreds of feeling like the big stuff you know you can be. Claw it out of the deepest part of you because if you give in and go down, it's not impossible, but it's a lot harder to come back up.

This is why I so strongly urge every business owner in this position to take bankruptcy off the table. Take bankruptcy off your table.

It's not to say it's not an option. It is, and it can seem easy in the position you're in right at this moment. It's not impossible to come back from bankruptcy, but why start to build back in the negative when you could start to build back from zero? Isn't zero better than negative 100?

Take Brandon. He was the sole owner of a multi-million dollar news website and e-commerce conglomerate. In the days of the Internet's Wild West era, where all you needed was a good mind for marketing and a store and a website to almost print money, he developed a way to duplicate his revenue over and over again.

By partnering with influencers (before that term existed) and other organizations, he developed a way to produce income for them and essentially took a cut, using e-commerce to grow the network, and ad revenue poured in from all sides. This company achieved Inc. 5000 placement, one of America's fastest growing privately held companies for 5 consecutive years.

Then in early 2017, this came to a dramatic halt. Overnight, ad revenue was cut more than 70% through the actions of an organization founded on venture capital out of Beijing and a US political advocate opposed to the general messaging of Brandon's company. Simultaneously, platforms used to drive traffic decided to severely limit reach, and even deleted pages with millions of followers.

This is one of those stories where perhaps an outside force involved itself in the downfall of a successful business, but the owner of this business is not completely left of the hook either.

He had let go of the reins. He had allowed his team to manage the business while he, shall we say, rested on his hard-earned laurels a bit. He didn't see the problems coming, but he might have, given the numerous warnings his financials would have provided if he had examined them daily.

But he was able to sell his business, granted at a much lower price than he had been offered a year prior. He managed to escape doom…for a little while. He built back a second company during 2018, a smaller scale version of what he'd had. He enjoyed the freedom and success of having sold a business he had built while developing new businesses and products.

The best of times, the worst of times. It's oft been said in the manufacturing industry that receiving an order from Walmart or Amazon can be the best or the worst thing that happens to you. In this case, it was the production of a product that got mentioned on a national and very popular television program that was the undoing of the business.

Overnight, orders increased by 1000%., and they didn't have enough product to fill the orders. They didn't have the fulfillment capacity to ship the product they had quickly enough. Being referenced on over 9 pages of Google search results was great for business and garnered even more orders — but product was being manufactured for delivery 4-5 weeks out and at Christmastime to boot.

All of this created an overnight challenge that seemed insurmountable. Any business owner who produces a product hopes and prays and works for this moment — and can be doomed by the very success that comes his way if he doesn't have the infrastructure that success necessitates.

Couple the production and fulfillment challenges with the unrealized promise of an SBA loan that was never approved, a bridge loan on the business's operations building that ballooned without means to repay, causing an immediate foreclosure, and the rushed tax return being filed for the SBA triggering an IRS audit, this situation would seem bad enough.

At the same time, he was opening a brick-and-mortar coffee shop for one of his divisions and found out the state laws had changed during his build-out and wouldn't allow any new business to roast coffee beans in the same facility it serves coffee. And he just financed a mac-daddy $115,000 roaster.

But wait…there's more.

In order to get production moving forward on delivering received orders, in order to keep building on the momentum of that one make-or-break moment in the news, and to build out the coffee shop that now has a massive and unusable liability on its books, multiple (and stacked) merchant cash advances had been taken out on the business. And the owner personally. And his wife. And his brother. And his business partner.

So, out of the blue, a buyer comes to rescue his business from utter collapse. Whew! In the nick of time to save Brandon from utter humiliation and business collapse, this buyer contractually obligates himself to several major liabilities, assumes ownership of the operations, and promptly defaults and disappears — with the assets that allow cashflow and revenue to come into the business.

Didn't see that coming! You can't serve a lawsuit to someone you can't locate, and you can't re-assume a business through breach of contract if you can't locate the assets!

One day Brandon is sipping cocktails on the paid-in-cash pool he put into his 8-acre estate during "the fat years," his paid-for RV parked on the cement pad out front of a manicured lawn, and a booked Presidential Suite 7-day cruise ahead.

The next day he's running down the hillside of his home in rural Georgia in his slippers and bathrobe to escape the early Saturday morning arrival of a sheriff trying to serve him papers from the merchant cash advances his business has been unable to service.

The roaster was reclaimed by the finance company. The warehouse he owned was foreclosed upon. The merchant cash advances immediately issued judgements against him and everyone he was connected to was harassed to get him to pay. His household estate was gone, and he moved his family into that RV to live for 9 months until they could afford to rent a home again.

Talk about humbling. Talk about losing your confidence, your swagger, and everything you thought you were. Talk about the feelings of guilt, desperation, even grief.

But here's where Brandon ended up. One day he's running away from the judgements. Another day he's spending money he doesn't really have to attend a fundraising dinner at The Jewel of Palm

Beach where he shakes the former President's hand…to the awe and astoundment of numerous clients. This results in securing another round of retainers for his consulting business, and he lives to fight another day.

Today, his business is gaining momentum once more, with a healthy measure of humility, a large dose of having learned from the past, and a very healthy measure of financial awareness from the boss. It would be too easy for someone facing bankruptcy on multiple fronts to say ok, I give in. Would he come back from it? Perhaps, in 7–10 years.

Instead, he fought and struggled and maintained that swagger long enough to dig out from the immense hole he found himself in just a mere 3 years ago.

This is what I mean when I say you cannot lose your swagger. Dig deep, find where it sits inside of your core, and don't let go of it. You cannot allow yourself to indulge in the five stages. You cannot allow yourself to wallow in grief, to despair, to live in a rage, to blame others or situations, and you most certainly cannot allow yourself to be overcome by fear. Fear is a f•cker. And fear *will* f•ck you. More on that in the next chapter.

The point is simple: if you allow grief, despair, or fear to control you, you lose your confidence (or as I call it: swagger), you lose that part of you that makes you, your business, your service, or product stand out.

If you hold on to that swagger, the ravenous collectors, the raging lenders, the angry vendors, and the hurt employees will not get you down so low that you can't rise back up.

You've perhaps heard of the self-help author Napoleon Hill and his most infamous title *Think and Grow Rich*. I don't personally hold to the idea that you can simply grow rich by thinking about it. However, let's discuss the concepts behind this somewhat revolutionary idea.

Hill, at the behest of Andrew Carnegie — the businessman, industrialist, and philanthropist who was then the richest man in the world — spent two decades conducting research in order to organize a Philosophy of Personal Achievement.

Armed only with a letter of introduction from Carnegie, the then-unknown journalist set out to interview over 500 people of the caliber of Henry Ford, Thomas Edison, Alexander Graham Bell, John D. Rockefeller, George Eastman, William Wrigley Jr., and Charles M. Schwab.

His discoveries include timeless success principles, many of which can be traced back to the ancient stoics who taught the greatest leaders of our time, such as:

- Start each day with an expression of gratitude.
- Don't allow yourself to be drawn into arguments over unimportant subjects.
- Exercise self-discipline over all of your emotions.

- Achieve self-mastery over your thoughts, and constantly direct them towards your goals and objectives.

- Master the negative habits which stand between you and success.

- Develop the positive habits you'll need in order to succeed.

- Acquire the habit of thinking before you speak.

These basic pointers have been utilized in the past by many greats and helped them to achieve their goals, and ultimately become icons of success for our generation today.

But the key point Hill makes that I want to share with you is this:

"Whenever you have a problem, concentrate your attention on the "can-do" portion of the problem. Then, begin to act where you stand and do what you can in order to solve the problem. Keep in mind that it doesn't matter what problem you may be having, or what you want to achieve, there is always something you can do right now that will help you. Find out what this something is, and do it." [3]

That's it! That's the ultimate goal of "getting back your swagger" in the likely most humbling time of your life, when you're at your lowest, and you feel out of control and like your business is spiraling down the toilet with you hanging on for dear life while everyone else is against you: that's when you absolutely must seek

---

3 https://daringtolivefully.com/napoleon-hill-success

the can-do portion of the problem and begin to act where you stand and do what you can in order to solve the problem.

And that, in a nutshell, is what I will help you do. Each day we will pull back the control you feel you've lost and, through small victories and seemingly tiny wins, we will bring back the swagger that you had, that confidence you exude that makes your business hum and your clients happy and makes your employees proud to work with you.

Then lastly, you'll put all you learned to good use. I don't work with people to get them out of the vortex and back into the sunny days of financial freedom to have them do it all again. In fact, I don't accept repeat clients!

My goal is that once you're back on top, you've learned from the mistakes you've made, grown from the challenges you've worked through, moved on from the battles you've fought, and you're never going to allow financial ignorance, excess of ego, or denial to bring down your business ever again.

You're going to learn from the Business 101 course you have just lived through. And most importantly, you're going to put into action some of the key ingredients that make a business successful and you'll never be *here* again.

QUIZ

But can *I* get out of this mess?

- Question 1: Am I willing to be open-minded to solutions?

- Question 2: Am I willing to fully trust and follow Joe's expertise and advice?

- Question 3: Am I willing to make necessary adjustments to my business so that it survives?

- Question 4: Am I willing to learn from this experience?

If you answered "yes" to one or more of these questions, the answer is YES. Now let's get started!

PART II

HOW DO I GET THROUGH THIS?

CHAPTER FIVE

FEAR WILL F*CK YOU

F ear is the ultimate enemy. Fear will f•ck you.

Fear kills more people than death. – George S. Patton, Jr.

Central to Patton's success in the theater of World War was his ability to control fear. Notice I did not say the absence of fear. In fact, during WWII, it is said that a military governor in Sicily met with Patton and commended him highly for his courage and bravery.

The story goes that Patton replied, "Sir, I am not a brave man ... The truth is, I am a coward. I have never been within the sound of gunshot or in sight of battle in my whole life that I wasn't so scared that I had sweat in the palms of my hands."

Years later, when Patton's autobiography was published, it contained this significant statement by the General, "I learned very early in my life never to let my *fears* take control of me."

What is fear? Fear is defined as dread, anxious concern, panic, terror, and an emotion based on anticipation.

While the fear of God or a prison sentence may keep some of us in line where we need to be kept in order to maintain societal norms of good behavior, the general concept of fear as an emotion of anticipated doom and potential ruin is what I speak against in this chapter.

The what-ifs will put you on a ledge. They will paralyze you right when you need to be moving into high-speed action. You may need to exert more action in the next few weeks of your life than ever, and if you're distracted by fear, you're going to inevitably find yourself freezing, pausing, holding back. You're going to take your foot off the gas pedal at the time when your business needs you pushing the petal to the metal the very most.

If you're in that state of fear, you're not going to be thinking clearly, positively, or even at all. There's a reason fear is considered a "primitive" emotion. You sense danger, you feel fear, you run from the danger, you're safe.

Challenge yourself to keep this primitive emotion of fear of "whatever could happen" because of the situation you're in right now at bay.

You may have to face it, and list out all the terrible things that could happen. Ok, now put that list away and get back to work. You may have to simply swipe right and keep it out of your mind completely. Ok, now get back to work. You might have to talk it out with me at 4am and hear the calm and reassuring voice on the other end of the phone that says, "It will be ok, we will get through this."

During fear, hormones flood the area of the brain known as the amygdala to help keep us alert and aware of the perceived threat, and our blood flows into the muscles that allow us to escape. Tackling fears helps our bodies get out of this stress response, allowing us to feel relief from both our triggers and their accompanying symptoms. Essentially, by controlling our fear we can begin to feel less fear.

Whatever it takes, you have to fight fear, because fear *will* f*ck you, your business, and your future.

"Never let the future disturb you," said Aurelius. "You will meet it, if you have to, with the same weapons of reason that today arm you against the present." Aurelius was fighting "barbarian" invasion, the Antonine plague, internal intrigue, and corruption, and all while it is suggested, through examination of his writings in what is essentially his diary *Meditations,* he was battling anxiety[4].

Franklin Roosevelt famously stated that we had nothing to fear but fear itself! And how true this statement rings, because many times in the end we find that our fears of what could happen were worse than what happened.

One of the most common denominators I see with business owners who are facing the darkest days of their life is that they all tell me, "Joe, I'm lying in bed at night and I can't sleep...."

---

4   https://www.thecollector.com/marcus-aurelius-meditations/

There's 1,001 issues, challenges, and what-ifs. But if your fear is getting the best of you and keeping you up at night, you've got another problem. Your health will start to fail. Your mental state will decline. When those go, the relationships that matter most can also suffer even more.

Instead we must lay hold of the advice that Marcus Aurelius gave us to "stay calm and serene regardless of what life throws at you." Sun Tzu wrote firmly: appear strong when you are weak!

Sun Tzu also pointed out that "If you wait by the river long enough, the bodies of your enemies will float by." How true this can be.

As I've pointed out previously, when you understand that time is your biggest asset, and I am able to buy you time, you'll often find that the proverbial bodies of your enemies will float past you.

For example, there was a very optimistic business owner and his wife who were drowning in a beautiful Western town known for high-end tourism. While the wife was selling real estate, the husband was spinning his wheels and losing his mind trying to keep the business appearing successful while it was buried in loans upwards of 1.5 million.

How do you convince an overly positive person that he should realize his utterly negative position while also coaching him to maintain his positivity? We couldn't have him lose their swagger, but if he didn't adjust his overly optimistic approach, he'd be losing his business.

The key was to buy time, and time we bought. Delving deep into the numbers (and numbers don't lie), we were able to connect with the owner and continually remind him of exactly where he stood financially. Through our coaching, we were able to let the spreadsheets speak for themselves, and bring him the numbers and tools he needed to get the business back on track financially.

And that time we bought them? It made all the difference. During the pandemic real estate boom, they were able to get their debt from $1.5 million to about $500,000, a number they can reasonably pay down and realize success in their future, not failure.

There are many examples in many books of fear f*cking up the world of emperors, commanders, authors, and business owners. Bankruptcy is the result of fear in just about 95% of all cases. Business owners who did not need to file for bankruptcy and put themselves and their businesses and their futures into a negative zone.

I've experienced clients filing bankruptcy within a week of contacting me to help them dig out; without fail it's because they faced fear, and fear overcame them.

A tech client about three months into the process had a great product. The plan was going well. The victories were coming… but he filed for bankruptcy. I was shocked and sad, but about a year later without asking he told me that if he had it to do over again, he would have blocked the fear that pushed him to bankruptcy. He wished he had taken my advice and pushed through the fear and not let it f*ck his business.

When I talk to a business owner, I have a plan and I give it to them. I quickly demonstrate that in my experience, the plan works every time if a client is committed to face the fear and push through it instead of letting it f*ck them over. I commit to them that if they are "in," I'll be in it with them. Bankruptcy costs so much more than fighting through the process, it destroys businesses, relationships, and disrupts family and future. But that door is always there; it's available later if there simply is no other option.

But in the majority of cases, I have found fear to be the reason business owners file for bankruptcy and fear can be controlled. My plan and process will help you fight that fear. Our path is on contingency, so what is the risk?

Sometimes you'll find the merchants or vendors pursuing you with such vigor one day are defunct the next. Creditors who cannot extract blood from a stone move on to other pastures. Hurt feelings and anger subside. Fear tells you they won't, but they will, and they do in time.

Again though, it takes more than time. It takes a person devoid of an excess of ego, who can trust the advice presented, and learn from their past. And control your fear at all costs.

When you get that 4am mind-churn, when you get the collection agency's latest nastygram, when your sister's ex-husband's cousin gets a call from a creditor trying to locate you and snidely lets you know, communicate to me, and let me help you through (and past) the fear cycle.

I've found that visiting my clients as much as possible helps to push back the fear, as well. So you'll find me on the road a lot of the year, checking in on my clients, talking them through the 4am mind-churn and the 4pm creditor calls. With our ability to get quick victories hours and days into the process, we build confidence and trust in both the process and yourself. Don't let fear control your decisions.

Fear is a f*cker. Don't let fear f*ck you!

CHAPTER SIX

BALANCING SWAGGER WITH HUMBLE TRUTH

I've talked a good bit about keeping up your confidence and not losing your swagger. I've also talked a bit about how an excess of ego can destroy your business like it has so many others.

It may seem like I've got a bit of a paradox here between exuding confidence and expressing humility.

Our society tends to teach us to power through. Men especially are taught to look tougher than you are, show no weakness, keep up the I of strength. Attorneys especially tend to push this mindset on the business owner struggling to keep up with liability payments and loans.

When the ground is crumbling beneath you is not the time to act terribly dignified or with hubris. It's a time to be real, to be honest, and to be humble with yourself, your family, your team, your creditors, and especially the consultants and advisors who you're hoping will help you.

Most entrepreneurs have a built-in swagger. It's a confidence, a level of optimism, that can-do attitude that made you step out into the frontier of business ownership sans a boss to tell you what to do, when to do it, how to do it, and take responsibility for the ultimate direction (and success or failure) of the business. Why work for someone else when I can do it better?

This can become (or perhaps is due to) hubris: that excess of ego that we've thoroughly described as a detriment to healthy, successful, and lasting businesses. After all, you've gotten this far, and you know what you're doing to some degree or you wouldn't have a successful business! You can handle it yourself.

Can I also point out that you've gotten here by yourself? And that "here" is not where you want to be! This over-optimism can be a coping mechanism, too, avoiding the reality of how bad the situation actually is right now. You don't want to look the problem straight in the face and understand realistically how hard it is going to be to dig out, and what you're going to have to do is not in off-chances and hoped-fors.

I see a lot of business owners who think they can get out of this mess on their own. They can work it out just fine. Or they call me and take half of my advice, but ultimately know better and end up in the same or a worse position.

Then they end up calling me when their ego folds into fear and they have nowhere else to go.

Don't be more willing to let that hubris, excess of ego, over-optimism or whatever you want to call it keep you in denial and keep you from accepting the humility of your current situation, and calling out for help. And call now.

If you don't call out now, it could be too late, or at the very least, so late that your climb back to the top is that much harder. If the theme of "time as an asset" has resonated with you at all during your journey through this book, perhaps remember that the sooner you call me, the sooner we can start working on getting you out of this hell and back on top.

I'm like a therapist for the business-owner. I'll call you down out of the clouds and point you to the reality of your situation, and realistically help guide you through it to the other side. Being over-optimistic or allowing that excess of ego to control is where you're going to think your numbers are lying. I can promise you that your numbers are not lying.

Example: Client: I'm going to call this long-term contact and he'll buy a million next month … they won't really foreclose on my house before that.

Joe: In reality, your house will be foreclosed in two weeks. You have the notice that says it's already happening. Why would this guy who's never bought from you for years buy so much from you (and pay you) now? Why are you lying to yourself?

Client: Silence. Then …you're right…

Joe: Now let's realistically determine the strategy…

At the same time, I've pointed out repeatedly that fear will destroy you and keep you from harnessing your brainpower and wits and creativity at the single most important time of your life. Losing your swagger, your confidence and allowing fear to control you can be as detrimental as excess of ego. It's a balancing act, and one that I will coach you through.

Confident people generally attract better results. Confident people are easy to work with, they are the fun ones at the work parties. Business owners with confidence tend to blaze trails, widen smiles, and bring positive energy wherever they float — and I say float because they tend to flit from room to room, person to person, spreading good vibes wherever they land.

Be objective, and we will balance the edifice of your confidence against the humility of the truth and through this balancing act of swagger and humility we can determine a strategy to come out on top.

One of the ways this is done is through an obsessive, almost compulsive plan of communication. Let's delve in.

CHAPTER SEVEN

IF CASHFLOW IS KING, COMMUNICATION IS QUEEN

People usually know when sh*t is hitting the fan. They might not know what fan or when or how fast the fan is going or what brand it is, but they have an innate sense of knowing when something is wrong and fun fact: they almost always assume the worst.

Instead of helping you look for solutions, Susie is now worried about her job and stressed about her bills and possibly looking for a new job on the clock instead of forging ahead with renewed confidence in her fearless leader who has shared so much with her and entrusts her with information that empowers her to help him find a solution.

Build trust and loyalty with your team by communicating what is going on. Verbalize the problems, the challenges, the issues, and ask for help in figuring out the solutions. Yes, this is part of that humility balancing act. It can be really tough to talk to your team about issues, potentially even failures that could affect them.

So many business owners, when faced with surmounting issues, think, "What I need is money!" True, but what you need even more is your army, armed and headed into battle with you. You have to exhibit the leadership that will make that team rally behind you and get through to the victory on the other side. Don't let your team think it's time to exit because they don't know anything else.

Be the visionary leader they chose to work for to begin with, be that fearless general who leads his troops through the battle. Don't wait until you cannot pay your team one week to tell them you're in trouble.

Key metrics and KPIs have to be established (by you) and communicated to your team, particularly your accounting team. If they know what makes the business a success or approaching a cliff, they'll be able to help you steer the ship instead of you going at it alone.

Leadership is not just about being out front and in charge. It's about rallying the team together and inspiring them. It's about letting them know that if they see anything or have any ideas, they can communicate to you because you will communicate to them also. There's also a unique phenomenon in coming out with full, honest, humble communication with your team in a time of struggle.

You might think your team will judge you or that they'll lose faith in you, but the opposite happens. You demonstrate leadership by communicating to your team openly, and you'll nearly always find their confidence in you and your ability has been bolstered. By trying to seem confident and hold back honest and open communication, you actually give them less reason to trust you, less confidence in you.

Teams that go through the fire together and come out on the other side tend to be stronger. You can look at any number of football teams or military divisions and find stories of how much stronger they were once "tested by fire" together.

In *The 21 Indispensable Qualities of a Leader,* John Maxwell points out that in our long history of presidential candidates, only one in our lifetime has been called the Great Communicator: Ronald Reagan.

Regardless of which side of the aisle your politics lean towards, no one can ignore the talent for communication that separated Reagan from many others in similar position. Throughout his career in radio, the movies, and finally, his most well-known role as the man who would end the Cold War, Reagan displayed an uncommon ability to connect and communicate.

The success of your marriage, jobs, relationships with friends and family members, and generally employees and coworkers, vendors and lenders relies on your ability to communicate. People do not follow you, go along with you, or trust you if your communication is lacking.

The first and most honest dialogue you need to start with is how you need your team. You cannot do this alone. You can't survive without them. Even if you started with no employees and it was just you, you've grown, evolved, developed, and built a company with a team of people now.

It doesn't matter if it's 2 people, or 200, or 2,000,000. Some might need to be cut due to sheer necessity or even perhaps incompetence, true; but it is also true that you cannot do battle without your collective troops. Communicate that to them. Be honest with about the company is in this moment. Good, bad, and ugly.

Generally, you'll find people will thank you for delivering bad news to them. They'd rather know facts than guess at worse news.

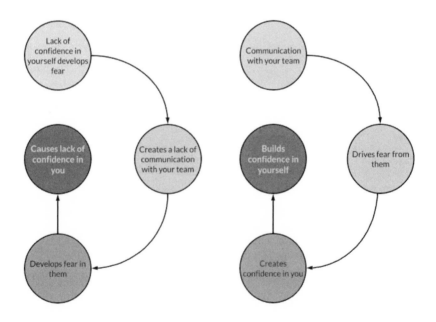

The second dialogue you're going to have to have is with your vendors. You're going to have to make it personal, and humble pie doesn't taste great but it's very likely going to buy you enough time to figure out how to pay them.

"We couldn't live without you." And this is true if you're in just about any business because, no matter what industry or line of work you're in, you have vendors who provide either services or products that you in turn sell to others or use to do your work.

Don't be too proud to say to your vendors, and honestly mean it: "You mean so much, I just wanted to tell you XYZ because you deserve to hear it from me now, we are so thankful for you, we 'ouldn't be here if you weren't a part of our lives."

From there comes the ask: "I need more time to pay. How much time can you give me?" And whatever they say, ask for a little more time and a little less cash. The worst thing they can do is say no, but you'll find, more times than not, they know you have to succeed in order for them to get paid.

Follow John Maxwell's advice: Simplify the message. See the person you're communicating to and connect with them. Show the truth; there is no greater credibility than to communicate truthfully. And seek a response: the best communicators give people something to feel, something to remember, and something to do.

When you have made the effort to be forthright and honest, communicate with your team and your vendors, you're much more likely to find them a part of your team striving to win the battle with you rather than either abandoning you at the worst time or demanding beyond your capabilities. Maxwell points out the simple truth: Without communicating, you travel alone.

CHAPTER EIGHT

TIME IS NOW YOUR BIGGEST ASSET

By now you've heard me say "time is an asset" repeatedly. Right at this moment, time could be your biggest asset.

You may be facing creditors repossessing your machinery, fleet, building, possibly even your family home. Banks may be freezing your accounts due to a judgment won against you. There have been those who have woken up to find their personal vehicles being towed away.

In 2011, Justin Timberlake, Amanda Seyfried, and a handful of other notables such as Cillian Murphy and Olivia Wilde, starred in a Science fiction film *In Time*, written, produced, and directed by Andrew Niccol. While critical acclaim eluded the dystopian drama where the primary currency of the year 2169 is a person's allotment of time on earth, Roger Ebert did give it 3 out of 4 thumbs up, a sign that it was definitely worth watching if for no other reason than to get your mind thinking about the concept.

With time transferred between parties in "capsules" as a barter for all necessities, we see the usual suspects: lenders of time; time-robbers. Banks hold vaults full of time. Casinos lay time on the table. The premise is somewhat terrifying, as we watch our protagonist race against his allotment to prove his innocence and end this system once and for all.

If we treated time with such value, perhaps our days would involve a little more learning and a little less social media. Perhaps our families would get a few extra capsules of time. We must learn to view time as our most valuable asset.

Equally, time is of the essence. This line is in the majority of contracts; particularly as it relates to the signing of a binding document, a "time is of the essence" clause spells out that inaction has an effect on the people or properties referenced. It can place urgency of timing on actionable items within the contract. And it is a definitely enforceable clause to the courts.

When determining whether "time is of the essence" from a contract, the court will look at the intent of the parties at the time they entered into the contract. *Steele v. Branch*, 40 Cal. 3 (1870). If there is an explicit clause in the contract stating that time is of the essence, the court will take that at face value and enforce it accordingly. *Martin v. Morgan*, 87 Cal. 203 (1890); *Leiter v. Handelsman*, 125 Cal.App.2d 243 (1954). Where time is of the essence of a contract, any failure to perform within the time specified is a material breach of the contract. *Gold Mining & Water Co. v. Swinerton*, 23 Cal. 2d 19, 27 (1943); *U. S. Hertz, Inc. v. Niobrara Farms*, 41 Cal.App.3d 68, 78 (1974). Put another way, where the parties provide that time is of the essence, they effectively agree that a breach of that promise is material or, in other words, that timely performance is in effect an express condition precedent to the other party's duty to render its own performance under the contract. 15 Williston on Contracts § 46:3 (4th Ed.); *Glock v. Howard & Wilson Colony Co.*, 123 Cal. 1 (1898).

Time is of the essence now, as you face the most difficult time of your life. I've yet to hear someone say to me, "Joe, I wish I had waited longer to call you." Quite the contrary, the sooner you call me the more of that valuable asset of time I can get for you.

Every day, every week that I'm able to buy you, that day or week means it's a little less likely your ship will completely sink or that your business will completely go under. Every day or week I buy you gives you the ability to keep your world that much more intact and gives you that much more opportunity to build back.

But you've got some work to do with this asset of time. You must learn how to prioritize your time, in the right ways. You must use your time to prioritize your financial awareness. You must use it to work out that financial muscle every single day. You'll need to focus on what will help your business in the best way at this moment.

It will be vital that you have a daily understanding of your business's health based on a few numbers that tell you "business is bad today, business is good today." These key indicators can come to you from your team, that team you've communicated with so well like we discussed before, and they've rallied as your army to help you solve the situation.

Every day, your key members are going to bring you the information you need to ascertain if your business has had a good day, an okay day, or a bad day.

Don't wait a month or two months to find out that last month put you in the negative. There will be key and simple measurements for every location, every department, every business that will help you know the exact health of your business today, and help you plan for tomorrow.

In my business, I look at things as simple as: how many emails came in and how many were answered? How many times have I spoken with each of my employees this week? How busy are they; how do they feel? What are they seeing as they interact with clients?

I check with my team internally as frequently as I'm able to see what their days are spent doing, what trends they're noticing, what they're experiencing. Oftentimes it will quirk a question in my mind that leads to either noticing a potential problem or results in an idea that boosts revenue.

Simple KPIs to give you an overall view of the health of your business is like getting a daily physical exam. Not checking on daily KPIs is like looking in the mirror. You see your image, but you have no idea if it's a healthy one. KPIs can vary based on industry and goals, even internal departments. Collectively they should give you a snapshot of the health of your business.

When you review simple daily KPIs, you're seeing your business's blood pressure, heart rate, glucose number, hydration levels. If you need to go get a deeper blood test or conduct majorly invasive surgery, you can delve deeper, but on a daily basis you just need a simple checkup to ensure the levels are normal.

Most business owners and entrepreneurs are 24/7, always focused on their business. It's not a question of spending time thinking about your business or working your business. You're already doing that! It's not a question of being busy: every business owner is busier than seems to be physically possible.

This is a plea to prioritize your time on the things that matter the most and can help your business the most in this hour. It may not be what you enjoy most. I've found that few entrepreneurs actually enjoy crunching numbers and examining spreadsheets; spending an hour a day reviewing numbers and formulas can seem like a century to the creative visionary that built a business out of nothing but an idea.

But that hour that entrepreneur spends giving his business a financial health exam can be the difference between another month in business or folding in complete failure wondering, "how could this happen?"

Good business owners are also continually looking for ways to get more: more time, more revenue, more good money. Many will focus on what they know best, often prioritizing sales and marketing. Why not? This has served in the past, after all; this is how you got your business off the ground most likely! But what if there's another outlet you haven't pursued?

For example, there was a business owner I tried to help who was that guy, always focused on his business. No complaints of an absentee boss here! But he was unable to redirect his time to pursue a just about guaranteed major Federal grant that could have helped his business tremendously. Instead, he prioritized something he enjoyed doing more than paperwork: bonding with existing clients.

There is nothing inherently wrong and everything right with building relationships with your clients! But at this moment in his business's life, he needed to look down the line and realize that the looming financial woes would not be held off by existing clients.

If he had spent the same amount of time pursuing this grant, he would have had more time to build his business and engage his clients without the strain and stress of financial negativity.

Your current situation may have left you with very little in the way of traditional assets, and you may feel like time has left you, too. Let's get busy now and start banking that asset of time together. Time is of the essence!

CHAPTER NINE

FINDING CONTROL IN THE CHAOS

Humans are wired to respond to short-term problems more easily than long-term ones, according to Harvard psychology professor Daniel Gilbert.[5]

Consider this simple example: a stray baseball lobbed towards your head causes an immediate reaction to duck. Something looming farther ahead with bigger consequences that requires dramatic and long-term adjustments to avoid — such as impending bankruptcy — can be harder to react to. Our bodies are wired with hormones to help us "fight or take flight," but they're less inclined to help us when we are faced with long-term chaos and crisis.

There's also a psychological toll in what is called "crisis fatigue." The year 2020 is a great example of crisis fatigue. Do you even recall

---

5   https://www.npr.org/templates/story/story.php?storyId=5530483

that we started that year obsessively discussing the unprecedented wildfires destroying Australia's outback?

When your business baby is spiraling into the abyss, creditors are knocking on every door they can find, and you are watching your life dissipate before your very eyes, it's painfully chaotic. Chances are that you picked up this book because of the chaos you're struggling through, and you very likely are experiencing crisis fatigue from the excess cortisol.

"Our bodi's can't sustain that level of nervous load," says Adrienne Heinz,[6] a clinical research psychologist at the National Center for PTSD, which is part of the US Department of Veterans Affairs. "Things start to fail, the wheels start to fall off. We experience a whole host of consequences — an uptick in anxiety and depression. You start to see insomnia, relationship distress."

With the time I'm able to get my clients, they're able to regain some control over the chaos. When they start to balance the humility of their situation with the swagger that builds confidence in themselves, and others in them, they start to regain control. When they communicate honestly and openly with the people that matter to them, they start to put themselves back in control of the situation, not the other way around.

It's not about the nickels and dimes you can rub together today, but holding onto the hope that your future holds a much higher rate of success than you're experiencing today.

---

6   https://www.wired.com/story/crisis-fatigue/

It's going to require you to dig deep, as I've stated a few times throughout this book. You didn't get here in a minute, and the solution won't take a minute either. But I'm here with you through the chaos, helping you to gain back control. Not with a quick fix that is a long-term detriment to your future like bankruptcy, but with the long-term adjustments and achievements that will render your future self happier, wealthier, and — hopefully — much wiser.

CHAPTER TEN

NUMBERS DON'T LIE: WHAT IS YOUR BOTTOM LINE?

The first step I recommend to every client will always be to figure out your numbers. Numbers don't lie. Numbers don't exaggerate or have unrealistic optimism. Z-Y will always equal X. X+Y will always equal Z.

What is the bottom line? You would perhaps be shocked at how many once-wildly successful business owners and entrepreneurs have no idea what their actual bottom line is week-to-week.

What are your non-negotiable expenses for this week?

What is a reasonable (not overly optimistic but a concise expectation) of revenue for the week? Fight against optimism in this situation and seek only realistic and reasonable numbers. On a bad week, what is the minimum you know your business will earn?

If the bottom line is negative, you must adjust until it is at the very least break-even.

"But I can..." protests the visionary entrepreneur who truly believes that he can pull a rabbit out of the hat.

In this situation I will always advise that you can only trust the numbers. If the numbers say you're going to end the week in the red, you're likely going to find yourself ending the week in the red. How long can your business survive ending weeks in the red? One year? One month?

Are you sure those expenses are actually non-negotiable? Have you communicated to that vendor / provider and asked for time, or is your ego standing in the way and costing your business time to pay that it desperately needs?

In my experience, I have found nearly every expense is negotiable. Creditors are like the big scary dog on the corner, and they bark and growl and bare their teeth in hopes you'll cower in fear and cave to their demands. With my expertise, you'll find their demands are negotiable down to pennies on the dollar. Leases can be negotiated. Vendor payments and debt schedules can be negotiated. Even payroll can be negotiable if hard decisions are made (more about this later).

What we end up finding is that most non-negotiable in the immediate are things like utility payments, payroll, and bare minimum costs to keep the business earning revenue, such as postage to ship orders for an e-commerce business or the produce and meat deliveries for a restaurant.

Putting these numbers on paper — even if digitally on Excel or a Google spreadsheet — gives you back a little bit of that control. This is your roadmap. You have these non-negotiable expenses going out and a reasonable expectation of this revenue coming in. Your bottom line may be $0, but it isn't -$10,000, either. Now take a deep breath and treat that roadmap like your Bible for the week. It's your guide, your crystal ball.

The future of your business relies upon you following this map religiously, like a workout plan your trainer has given to get off those extra pounds before the wedding or beach trip. Every week you create a new map. Perhaps you have the ability to start working farther out, a month at a time. Regardless of how much money comes in or comes out, the key is to trust the numbers, because the numbers don't lie.

One of my first big clients was a young couple with two small children and a small chain of high-end retail shops in the greater Boston area.

Growth had been an enemy; between the expense of building new locations and stocking them with inventory, they didn't know where to turn but to fast financing: cash advance loans that were sucking 80% of their gross revenue.

With over $5 million in debt to 21 creditors, this young couple was facing failure and rapidly. I remember being so angry at the predatory actions these creditors used against them. The wife looked as though she had not slept in days. Her husband told me story after story of being personally threatened and referenced actions I knew were law-breakers from these predatory lenders.

I'll never forget how angry I was, and I let my emotions get the best of all of us. Numbers don't lie, and I was too upset that this family was facing failure to notice the numbers said this business was already too far gone to save. They did unfortunately close down for good, but not until I had put over $350,000 of my own funds into a business that did not have enough reasonable revenue to balance out its non-negotiable expenses.

This was a time I did not follow my own advice and stick to trusting the numbers. But there's a not terrible ending to this story. Despite being personally liable for over $5 million dollars, they own both their homes and maintain their family.

I had put myself in the other person's shoes and felt their fear and stress, "oh my God, what am I going to do?", but if I put myself on the other side of the equation, and I was hands on, I could have made it work. There was so much debt that the creditors were willing to accept next to nothing. They see you as so uncollectable that they're willing to accept pennies on the dollar.

CHAPTER ELEVEN

PUT YOUR PLANNING ON STEROIDS

When I was 19, I started my first business selling ink cartridges when laser printers were the new boom in technology. Managing to net a government contract with the Navy base in Norfolk, I was able to get used cartridges for half the cost, and after recycling, I was finding revenue far outperforming costs.

Ultimately that business failed because I had no control over the quality process of recycling. But in the meantime, it helped to pay my way through a finance degree from William & Mary.

But being an entrepreneur was what I planned to be; it's what I was good at and always found myself gravitating towards. Between 1989 and 2000 I was working for myself and building an investment firm.

I was single, no kids, no mortgage, no real responsibilities. I did what I want. Why not? Planning is something you do when you're worried about your estate towards the end of your life, right?

Being Joe, Inc., I had never really needed to take measures to plan out this real business, its growth, its structure, its potential pitfalls, its need to provide a future. And then I got married and had two kids.

Immediately I realized that you have to plan, plan, and plan some more. Plan ahead, rethink the plan, communicate the plan, you know the drill. Suddenly this business has to provide not only for me, but for three others, and long-term it has to exist even without me. What if I'm gone? Will my family be able to survive financially?

This was a life-changing pivot, and I urge you to take another look at whatever business you're in right now and put your planning on steroids. It's never too late to plan, but planning in advance is far preferable to planning under the strain and stress of absolute necessity — or worse, putting off planning until it's actually too late to do it.

I discovered, during those pivotal moments when I determined to seriously plan for my business's long-term survival, that my business had all the trappings of success; but without a plan, it had no direction. And without direction, businesses are lost.

Yes, I was the only investor, I had no bank debt, revenues were strong, and it was growing. I was hiring more people, and we were doing more business than ever. But I hadn't been looking at my financials the right way. I wasn't studying my numbers and realizing that in our transactional business model, if just one of our large transactions disappeared, we would lose a major chunk of our business.

And that is exactly what happened when the financial crisis of 2007–2008 hit.

Overnight, or at least over the course of a very fast 6 months, my business was more than halved.

But I had begun planning! While my investment firm was 75–80% of my business, I had started to build up a stock certificate transfer agency.

It's true that digital transactions largely dominate the industry, but even today, there remains a need for an agency to process various activities as it relates to paper stock certificates. This is the kind of sticky business you might call "mailbox money." Though highly regulated, this business is relatively simple to manage, and clients rarely leave your service once gained.

While my investment firm halved, and quickly, my "side" planning began to deliver. Sure, it wasn't as sexy. It's not as exciting to have a large volume of small transactions versus a small number of large transactions, but the beauty of mailbox money is that you learn that planning ahead can save the day.

It isn't about the fancy titles, the nicer offices. These superficialities can seem to be signs of success, but they can be distractions that keep you from paying attention and planning ahead. Don't let the shiny distract your eye so that your focus is on what is working currently instead of looking ahead to that what-if should the current situation change.

We could talk all day about businesses that have not planned ahead for changes or crises. Radio Shack could have been the Amazon of online retail for all things electronic. Instead, they didn't plan ahead to a world where people no longer went to a retail store to buy wires and cords.

Blockbuster could have planned ahead to a world where you didn't just have one movie at a time to watch, but millions of hours of content suggested by algorithms based on the percentage ratio of enjoyment of other content you've watched.

Walgreens, on the other hand, could have gone the route of a number of other small family-owned pharmacies and disappeared from memory instead of being a nearly every corner landmark in every partly populated area of the country. Their biggest competitor in the 1990's was Eckerd ... where are they now? Drugstore.com was a short-lived competitor. Where are they now? Walgreens embraced technology, the internet, made good hiring decisions, and a focus on productivity over hours worked has made them a national icon that has far out-performed the majority of their competition.

In bad times, plan A rarely ever works out. Plan B oftentimes doesn't either. You'll often find your saving grace in Plan C, D, or even E. And remember that sometimes the game of business is not about being better than the guy next to you, but outlasting him.

Situations can be like erosion, or they can be like landslides. You may not always notice erosion, and you may not be able to stop a landslide. But you can plan for how you handle either. You can plan how you'll stay in business longer than your competition.

How are you prepared to face the inevitable rate of inflation or increase in taxation? How are you prepared for unexpected catastrophes like 2001, 2008, or 2020 brought businesses?

Even unavoidable traumas like the loss of a loved one, or a divorce, or the illness of a child can disrupt operations dramatically, and for good reason, and if you have no plan in place for the what-ifs, they'll eventually find you and possibly threaten your success.

The Los Angeles restaurant owner who experiences solid reservations every day of the week ... until a pandemic and government-ordered lockdowns closes business for months, then permanently.[7]

The business owner who doesn't plan ahead will find himself too slow to cut costs, or payroll, if necessary to the survival of the business. You must hone your ability to pivot, and pivoting requires planning.

Let's look at the other side of the coin now. Most businesses that are not growing will eventually be passed by competitors or face

---

7   https://la.eater.com/2020/5/8/21252137/los-angeles-la-restaurant-bar-permanently-closed-coronavirus-crisis-pandemic

flatlining from sheer insignificance. What is your plan for growth? Does your team know about it?

What will make you outlast your competitors? What will keep your clients with you and not seeking another option? What will make your business last through economic downturns?

Put your planning sessions on steroids. If you plan once a year or once a quarter, prioritize finding the time to double those planning sessions. Everything is cyclical, and there's nothing that proves this more than history. The one constant is that you cannot avoid everything, but you *can* plan for anything.

When you're busy working in your business, it can be difficult to see ahead and plan. The business owner who is always on the phone closing deals, always creating a new marketing email, always building relationships with employees and clients, always focusing on the financials, and seeking to increase revenue will have to make the effort to stop all the busy work to focus on planning.

Prioritize times when you can zoom out and look ahead, absorb industry news that could affect your future, develop what-if scenarios and how your business can respond, pivot, adjust, and survive. You might find you sleep better at night, too, if you know how you will handle the unknown when it hits you because you planned for it or a situation like it.

How will your business outlast the competitors? How will your business face a financial downturn or a new regulation that affects your specific corner of the market? How quickly can you pivot?

Write down the 3-5 worst things that could happen and make 3–5 plans for getting through them. Don't find yourself facing the unknown without a plan. Put your planning on steroids and have a plan in place.

Then revisit it every few months; review and revise as necessary. Every day you should be thinking about what you can do to plan for what could happen so that if it does, you're in control.

CHAPTER TWELVE

YES, YOU CAN

W e've discussed open honest communication even when it is humbling. We've discussed holding onto your swagger when the odds are completely against you having anything to be confident about.

We've delved into the absolute necessity to work out your financial muscles and know your bottom line doesn't lie. We've talked about time being your greatest asset, perhaps your only liquid asset at the moment.

And we have stressed the importance of planning for the one constant in life: change.

And we've talked a lot about the chaos, crisis, and cortisol you're experiencing in your life right now and how important it is that you hang on to hope and start working on how to get out of this mess, and more than that even, to build back even better.

If you're like a lot of people, you've been groaning repeatedly, "I can't."

Yes. You can. You must.

The temptation for many humans is to give in, to curl up in the fetal position and beg for a quick and merciful death. Bankruptcy is often the first idea, even suggestion, that many business owners get when faced with seemingly insurmountable financial difficulties.

In my experience, nearly every business is salvageable. Either the problems are fixable if we start in time, or through adjustments and creativity, we can find solutions to salvage your business and your future life. Nearly everything is negotiable.

Bankruptcy sounds to many like a tough, hard, terrible decision, but oftentimes it can feel like the quickest and easiest solution to your woes. Creditors will have to leave you alone. Vendors will have to stand in line. The temptation to surrender is strong, sometimes stronger than perhaps your will to fight the battle for a few more months in hopes that you can come out as a victor on the other side.

Waiting a few more days could be all the difference. Take the battle of Bastogne as an example.

For days in a snow-buried December, American troops battled German forces in the town of Bastogne. It was Christmastime, 1944.

It was freezing cold, food was running out, and medicine was nearly gone. The three-story hospital was bursting at the seams. A chaplain was holding Christmas services in the stables when the scream of a bomb landing on the hospital decimated morale even further.

This week marked in history the biggest and most deadly single battle of World War II. Nine days before, outnumbered Americans had been assailed and defeated by German troops and armory. 23,000 American troops were captured; 47,500 had been wounded and over 19,000 killed.

Belgian citizens had not been spared, either. A Catholic priest was murdered and a man who had hidden a homemade American flag in his basement was beaten to death by the Nazis. The battle between the sieging Germans and American troops barely holding onto the city continued without a seeming end.

Turrets in armored vehicles froze in place. Soldiers were freezing to death in foxholes. Ammo was running out, too, and help from the air wasn't coming due to the harsh weather conditions.

"The snow must turn red with American blood," one German soldier wrote to his wife of the situation. "Victory was never as close as it is now."

Outgunned, outnumbered, under-clothed and lacking basic necessities, it might seem that Brig. Gen. Anthony McAuliffe should accept "fate" and evacuate the American troops from the city and let the Germans have it. Evacuate now and let the enemy have the ground; perhaps it would be easier and less bloody than holding on a little longer.

The Germans issued a demand for surrender. McAuliffe was awakened by Lt. Colonel Moore. "The Germans have sent some people forward to take our surrender," Moore told him.

McAuliffe, still half-asleep and climbing out of his sleeping bag, said "They want to surrender?"

"No sir, they want *us* to surrender," replied Lt. Col. Harry Kinnard.

The general laughed. "Us surrender, aw nuts!" he said, before dropping the message on the floor.

This legendary history lesson continues on for a while, but the end point is that the Germans eventually got his response to their demand for surrender of the city.

"NUTS," was all it said.

"What does this mean?" the Germans asked. A medic who spoke German was told to say it basically meant: "Tell them to take a flying shit!" Instead, he turned and faced the Germans. "Du kannst zum Teufel gehen," telling them they could go to hell.

There was no surrender.

McAuliffe inspired his soldiers even further with a Christmas Eve message to his troops that explained the situation.

"What's Merry about all this, you ask? We're fighting — it's cold, we aren't home. All true, but what has the proud Eagle Division accomplished with its worthy comrades the 10th Armored Division, the 705th Tank Destroyer Battalion and all the rest? Just this: We have stopped cold everything that has been thrown at us," McAuliffe wrote on Dec. 24, sharing the German surrender message and his response with the division.

"We are giving our country and our loved ones at home a worthy Christmas present and being privileged to take part in this gallant feat of arms are truly making for ourselves a Merry Christmas."

The siege was finally broken on Dec. 26 after elements of General George Patton's Third Army arrived in Bastogne from the southwest.

It was considered a turning point of the war against Nazi Germany. Churchill said, "This is undoubtedly the greatest American battle of the war and will, I believe, be regarded as an ever-famous American victory."

I won't lie to you that it will require a lot of stamina, and out-of-the-box thinking. It will take more grit and determination and guts than you may think you hold. It may take major adjustments in your operations, thinking, and actions. It may involve difficult decisions to cut staff you might not think you can live without.

But nearly every business is salvageable and I will be there every step of the way, helping you through the entire process, like your fitness trainer, helping you see your financials properly, helping you develop the plan, bringing calm to your chaos by buying you time to make it another day. Even if your business is the rarity that may be "unsalvageable," you will find it to be far superior to start rebuilding at ground zero than to start from the negative 100 of bankruptcy.

The biggest mistake you can make is waiting too long to call. Call now so we can get you through this and on to rebuilding a stronger and better future.

PART III

HOW DO I REBUILD AGAIN?

CHAPTER THIRTEEN

REBUILDING STRONGER AND BETTER

M any business owners know what made their business successful at the beginning. Frequently you'll find that they started it all themselves. The capital account started with blood, sweat, tears, and likely their life savings or at least all the funding they could scrounge together when they started "Individual, Inc."

Over time, of course, they've developed and evolved. Their business likely grew, added employees, departments, possibly even locations. Was it because of good selling? Was it because they had a corner of the market with few or no competitors? Was it because they built relationships with the right clientele?

The restaurateur that has "the best hamburger in town" or the e-commerce marketer who has the coolest new novelty item and the owner of a steel beam manufacturing plant who has the biggest government contract in the country must all share the same thing if they want to remain in business: they have to know how to run a business!

It's not just about passion, vision, or strong salesmanship. You have to know how to run a business! Having a passion for good cheeseburgers or knowing the process for getting steel beams from one end of the country to another or knowing just the right catch phrase to sell out of a novelty item are not going to forever result in a business growing or even surviving.

Over the past pages, I have talked a lot about understanding your business's financials, developing plans, and making tough decisions to keep the business on track. All of these are part of "knowing how to run a business," but there are three core principles that really set you apart from the guys who have a business and those who know how to run a successful business.

These are the same three principles that I suggest will help you to rebuild stronger and better as you find yourself getting through the toughest challenge of your life.

Trust

- Trust my expertise and follow my instructions fully.
- Work on building trust with your team.
- Don't lead with greed.

Communication

- Foster open and honest communication with your team, vendors, and providers.

- Invest in realistic and frequent communication with your accounting team.

- Communicate your growth plans for full buy-in.

Discipline

- Stick to the plan we develop.

- Work out your financial muscles daily.

- Develop backup plans for your backup plans.

Let's discuss.

I've frequently used the metaphor of a fitness trainer giving a workout plan that brings those extra pounds under control, gets you fit and healthy, back in shape and ready to dominate the marathon ahead of you. I consider myself to be that fitness trainer for you and for your business.

This takes trust, and I acknowledge that you may not know me from the next guy, but I commit to you that I will work with you, help you, guide you, and your trust in me and my advice will get you where you need to be. Follow the plan, listen to my advice, and let my expertise work for you.

Expect direct and honest communication, even to the point where you might say I was "brutal." For example, I was talking to a guy in Pittsburgh. I could hear the fear in his voice, masked with bravado. He is a business owner who has 2 painful cash advances stacked against his revenue. He's about to file bankruptcy.

And I had to be brutally honest in my communication to him: Stop it. Get out of your head. Stop fearing the possibilities and let's tackle the problem to get you back on track. He completely had a positive outcome possible, but the fear of the unknown was making him believe putting himself into a worse position was the better option.

In Virginia, a small manufacturing company had taken four cash advances simultaneously in 2017, and his revenue of $2 million was struggling to cover the repayments on that $400,000. We settled for 50% on the dollar and got him the necessary time to pay that. Since then, he's been able to restructure, with all manufacturing now done in-house. His revenue has doubled and he has zero cash advances today.

Another client in Southern California was about to go out of business after over 30 years of success, due to the burden of seven cash advances crushing his clothing manufacturing company. His attorney had advised him to file for bankruptcy. At 80 years old, this was not someone who was going to have the retirement he had dreamed of, and that weighed on him. We mapped a different route. His business is now stronger than ever before, after we helped him settle all seven cash advances for pennies on the dollar.

Trust me. Listen to my advice. Follow our plan. Let my expertise work for you. My job is to be here until you don't need me anymore. I will be honest and open with you, and we will work together to get you back on track.

At the same time, we will work on building trust with your team with open and honest communication. Develop relationships with the people who keep your business running. You are likely the visionary, the leader who has to show them that working with you is for a purpose. Develop and share mission statements, values, goals.

Show your team that you entrust them with the day-to-day and that you're with them on the front lines. No one wants an absentee boss who leaves the hard decisions for another day, nor do they want the micromanager who demands they adhere to SOPs that are inefficient or outdated. Build trust with your team by being involved and aware and honest.

Trust is created by actions. Words like "best" or "the most" or "the biggest" are everywhere: we call them marketing. Actions create trust and if you seek trust not transactions, your success rate will be much higher.

I have two clients I've worked with over the past few years. We'll start with a cautionary tale. A commercial contracting business out of a major city experienced a measure of success in digging out of a mess. Things were looking great, and the owner got a little cocky. He decided to ignore some of my advice and start looking for easier ways to get out of his pickle.

Instead of focusing on good service to his existing customers and building trust with them, he spent his time — and cash — chasing major contracts with leads that didn't turn into customers. As his existing customers began realizing how little attention they were receiving, they would fire him. He spun his wheels chasing after "bigger, better, easier" jobs instead of focusing on the right kind of jobs. Eventually this greed and lack of trust-building with his customers would sadly send his business and personal life into bankruptcy.

On the other side of the country, the owner of a solar installation company in California is focused so strongly on people, helping them, connecting with them, that I've never seen so many people who will go the extra mile in return. Not just employees or vendors, but outside sales organizations! His genuine and sincere interaction with every person he meets builds such trust and loyalty that the business has experienced unbelievable growth: from $6 million in annual revenue to $6 million per month.

A lack of trust fosters fear. Fear can develop into greed.

Which leads us to my second point, don't lead with greed. There will always be someone who can outperform, underprice, overperform, or outshine you. Don't let them compete with how you treat your employees, your clients, and your vendors. If you treat people well, they'll treat you well in return.

Of course, this demands the caveat "in most cases." There are always exceptions that render the phrase, "no good deed goes unpunished" valid. At least in those cases, you know you did the right thing even if they did not.

Greed has caused billions of dollars to be squandered in the past few decades alone. The "10 worst cases of corporate greed[8] in the USA" lists the Lehman Brothers scandal, the Enron debacle, Bernie Madoff and Worldcom — all household names and tales of criminal charges, and many others that at the very least demonstrate a great deal of unethical patterns.

At the foundation of all of these scandals: leaders who let greed control them. Greed is the opposite of generosity. True generosity comes from the heart, with sincerity and genuine desire to give something back to the world. It's not an event, it's a pattern of life, as demonstrated by many of the empirical business greats in the past such as Andrew Carnegie, J.P. Morgan, Andrew Mellon. In more recent history, Warren Buffett, Michael and Susan Dell, Eli and Edythe Broad, and Charles Koch are some of the world's highest-giving philanthropists.

Generosity regards money as a resource, not as the ultimate goal. Obviously, you and your business and all of us are seeking to earn a living, and hopefully a comfortable one! But as Andrew Carnegie wrote in his 1889 essay, the life of a person should involve two periods of time: one in which they acquire wealth and the second in which they redistribute their wealth to others. Devoid of generosity, and the cultivation of generosity as a pattern, we find greed.

---

8   https://www.investmentzen.com/
    news/10-worst-cases-of-corporate-greed-in-us-history

Greed is ultimately a lack of restraint: oftentimes a lack of ethical restraint, and some might even call it moral restraint. A lack of restraint is the opposite of discipline, and discipline is one of the core "Indispensable qualities of a leader," as referenced in John Maxwell's book of the same title.

"To conquer oneself is the best and noblest victory; to be vanquished by one's own nature is the worst and most ignoble defeat," wrote Plato. Author Mike Delaney has aptly remarked that, "Any business or industry that pays equal rewards to its goof-offs and its eager-beavers sooner or later will find itself with more goof-offs than eager beavers."

The infamous car company created by former GM employee John DeLorean is a cult icon, particularly to anyone who lived through Back to the Future on the big screen. His rise to seeming success was at the expense of the discipline that GM had staunchly held its team to.

But instead of a creative environment bursting with energy and a sanctuary for the creative soul, DeLorean's company was dysfunctional, over-political internally, and even corrupt. Eventually, this flouting of conventional wisdom and complete lack of discipline rendered a collapse as heavy as the futuristic car itself. The company imploded, but only after resorting to criminality, fraud, and a loss of around $250 million.

Instead of improving on a system, DeLorean threw the system out. Instead of fostering creativity through structured energy,

DeLorean spat out the entire concept of structure and the result was chaos.

Instill discipline within yourself. This can be especially difficult for the visionary entrepreneur who is of a more creative nature, someone who chafes at studying those financials and would much rather be wining and dining a potential client than sitting in four walls mapping out the week's expenses.

You'll have to learn to fight for discipline. Sun Tzu is attributed with pointing out that a non-observance of discipline is one of the six ways to court defeat. Paraphrased: The leader strictly adheres to discipline; thus it is in his power to control success.

Marcus Aurelius dug deep into the topic of discipline also:

"At dawn, when you have trouble getting out of bed, tell yourself: 'I have to go to work—as a human being. What do I have to complain of, if I'm going to do what I was born for—the things I was brought into the world to do? Or is this what I was created for? To huddle under the blankets and stay warm?

'—But it's nicer here…'

So you were born to feel 'nice'? Instead of doing things and experiencing them? Don't you see the plants, the birds, the ants and spiders and bees going about their individual tasks, putting the world in order, as best they can? And you're not willing to do your job as a human being? Why aren't you running to do what your nature demands?

'—But we have to sleep sometime…'

Agreed. But nature set a limit on that—as it did on eating and drinking. And you're over the limit. You've had more than enough of that. But not of working. There you're still below your quota. You don't love yourself enough. Or you'd love your nature too, and what it demands of you. People who love what they do wear themselves down doing it, they even forget to wash or eat.

Do you have less respect for your own nature than the engraver does for engraving, the dancer for dance, the miser for money or the social climber for status? When they're really possessed by what they do, they'd rather stop eating and sleeping than give up practicing their arts."

This discipline is what will give you the willpower to study those financials. To plan ahead. To do the hard things and make the difficult decisions. It will keep you working on the plan, and help you realize success long-term.

One way to school yourself in the art of discipline is to read one chapter of a book on any topic that does not particularly interest you every day and write one sentence about it in a journal. Another method could be to schedule a 5-minute workout (run around the block, do 20 pushups, even breathing exercises) into your morning or evening routines.

Other suggestions have included setting — and sticking to — a series of small goals: every day this week I will eat one meal devoid of _____ (sugar or carbs, for example).

Whatever you decide to incorporate into your life, maintain it for 21 days, which develops your "habit" muscle. It can also be important to think of yourself as becoming a disciplined person through the process, rather than that you are denying yourself of something.

Small and incremental steps towards developing your self-discipline will go a long way in creating lasting success overall, and particularly where it involves your business. Sort out your priorities, establish your goals, stick to your values, crush your excuses, and create habits that will serve to cultivate discipline in your personal life. It will naturally serve your professional life as well.

In his iconic classic business tome *Good to Great,* Jim Collins points out that people who have learned to discipline their minds make the best leaders. While a highly capable person can deliver productive contributions through their talent or skills, and while a manager may be competent at organizing people and processes to produce results, it is the "paradoxical blend of personal humility and professional will" that "builds enduring greatness" and makes for the best leaders.

CHAPTER FOURTEEN

OWN EVERY ASPECT OF YOUR BUSINESS

" **B**ut that's Susie's job, I don't know...."

"Chuck's the one who handles that...."

"I'm not sure, I need to ask...."

These are the kind of commonplace statements I get from so many business owners who have come on hard times, and I still can't help but raise my eyebrows and shake my head. How can you purport to know your business if you don't actually know your business?

Does it mean you have to actually physically attach wickets to wockets? No. Does it mean you have to be the only person who balances the books or writes the replies to Yelp comments? No. But you should know how to do it. You should own every aspect of your business, or it will likely own you.

That employee you trust explicitly could leave your employment suddenly, by choice or perhaps, God forbid, not. One of my clients had a manager who handled 90% of every aspect of the business; one night he was tragically killed instantly in a car accident on the way home from work.

The business floundered for months as the owner tried to figure out how to do basic functions, fill out necessary paperwork, learn processes required for the regulated industry they were in. All because the owner stepped out and let the manager hold the responsibility for nearly every aspect. The business owner ended up losing quite a bit of investment due to the loss of the person who truly owned every aspect of the business.

While it may seem unlikely that your MVP will pass suddenly in a car accident or quit without passing on processes, procedures, and passwords, it would probably shock you how many times I have observed a floundering business as the owner says over and over, "I don't know … " to many of the most basic questions.

It's not wrong to not know; it's wrong to keep going in your ignorance. Learn everything. Know how everything is done, how everything works, how to make the business keep spinning if you were the only person running it.

Your business is a living, breathing organism. Every day it is getting stronger or it's getting weaker. It's getting bigger, better, or shrinking. You should own every aspect of your business to the point that you notice the slightest twitch or irregular heartbeat or rise in blood pressure.

Business owners and entrepreneurs tend to pick areas they like to work on, and who doesn't? We may know that part of the business very, very well. What about the areas you don't particularly enjoy? What about the roles you've been very happy to pass off to Susie or Chuck? If you own a business, you should own every aspect of that business.

Sure, you may have started the business and perhaps it was at one time only you keeping it spinning. What about now? Or perhaps you are working deep into a specific area … what about the other dozen areas?

Again, I'm not suggesting that you have to actually complete each and every task yourself, no, we'll talk more about hiring the right people for the right seats, especially as you realize the growth you want your business to achieve. But you absolutely should know how everything runs in your own company, and know how to measure the health of it day-to-day.

And it may not always be in the numbers; if you're buried so deep into only the financials that you don't notice the ebb and flow of customer satisfaction or the slowing of effective advertising, you may find yourself 9 months down the road wondering what happened. If you're involved in owning every aspect of your business, you'll have a much better chance of catching detrimental trends before they go unnoticed for months.

Another situation I too frequently find is a business owner who knows someone has to go, but they're afraid to actually act because "Who will do ____'s job?" The minute someone becomes a problem, they need to go. If you've given them good, clear, and honest feedback that has been ignored, or the repeated requests for performance alterations to occur have gone uncommitted, it's time to make the cut.

If someone has so much control you can't do anything about them, something has to change immediately.

The business does not have room for dead weight. It cannot carry people with it, especially if it's struggling or seeking to grow.

Don't be caught off guard by life's curve-balls. Plan ahead and own every aspect of your business. Own all aspects of your business so that if someone goes unexpectedly or has to be sent away, you're in control.

CHAPTER FIFTEEN

DEVELOP A LONG-TERM PERSPECTIVE

W hile we've spent a great deal of time talking through the day-to-day examination of your financials, the open and constant communication with your team that is necessary, and the moment-by-moment chaos you've found yourself coming through, now is the time to discuss putting one eye on your long-term goals.

"The future belongs to those who see possibilities before they become obvious," said the former CEO of Pepsi and Apple Computer, John Sculley. Examples of pioneers we admire for their long-term vision include Walt Disney, Steve Jobs, and Robert Woodruff, the president of Coca-Cola for over 30 years, who was responsible for turning the drugstore novelty into a globally adored brand.

These greats saw possibilities the rest of the world would only see once they were on the big screen of the movie theaters, or the small screen of the iPhone, or painted on the side of a building in your favorite downtown.

When you think of Walt Disney, you may think of Mickey Mouse or the many hundreds of movies favorited by children globally every year. But Walt's ultimate long-term vision was Disneyland. And he spent an extraordinary amount of time thinking, planning, and executing his idea for Disneyland. Engineer Rolly Crump shared some insight:

"In designing for Disneyland you definitely worked more as a conduit for Walt's ideas. He directed what you were doing, and his direction was far superior to your own personal ideas. His ideas were way ahead of yours — you had to play catch-up on that, and then you had to kind of read subconsciously what it was that he wanted and the direction to take. Walt would come up with an idea, and that idea would explode inside of him. It would get better and better. So when you showed him something, he would take what you did to another level. And when you gave it back, he'd take it to yet another level."

Walt was already ahead of newly presented ideas. His vision was of a future possibility that was not yet obvious to the rest of the world.

Long-term perspective — otherwise known as your vision for your future, and the future of your business — is vital to your business's success now.

Where there is no vision, the people perish, says the biblical proverb. Conversely, where there is vision, there is also a magnetic draw.

Your vision for the future will attract others like a magnet: people who will be drawn to you and your business. Employees who will help you get there. Financiers, mentors, customers, and other resources will come to you. Success will latch on to success. Your ability to see the possibilities ahead of you before they become obvious to others will lead you to greater success than you realize now.

What is the most important combination? Long-term perspective married to effort. I do not believe we can simply speak into the ether and obtain great success / wealth / happiness. It takes effort, which reminds us of the absolute necessity of self-discipline.

For example, 27-year-old fax machine salesgirl Sara Blakely took her life savings of $5,000 and an idea, and got rejected by every hosiery mill in the industry capital. But when one finally accepted her idea, she packed and shipped every order, and wrote her own patent application and grew shapewear into a billion-dollar (plus) niche.

A penniless single mom named Joanne Rowling was struggling with depression when she wrote to that 13th publisher and became the first author to earn over a billion dollars, and all within a mere twenty +/- years. Another well-known author, Stephen King, was rejected 30 times!

Van Gogh never stopped painting, though in his lifetime he sold just one painting to a friend for very little money. Steven Spielberg was rejected not once, not twice, but three times from USC's School of Theater, Film and Television. Michael Jordan was cut from his high school basketball team.

Persistence, determination, grit, whatever you want to pull out of yourself to see five, ten, or twenty years down the road, it's that long-term perspective that keeps those qualities sharp and honed in your gut and keeps you working hard to achieve those goals.

It's a long-term perspective that sees forward and understands that short-term thinking won't develop long-term success.

Now plan it out. Write it down. Put the "Big Hairy Audacious Goals" to paper and work on communicating this vision for your future to your team. And with that will come some decisions.

It's time to shift from spending every minute eying your next step and start seeing the possibilities of your future. Are you ready to experience life with a long-term perspective?

CHAPTER SIXTEEN

HIRE FOR THE GROWTH YOU DREAM

O ne of the first things I notice with many entrepreneurs and business owners is how long members of their core team have been on their payroll. "Susie's been here since the beginning!" "Chuck's been my right-hand man for 25 years!"

With long-term staff comes loyalty, usually and hopefully from both sides. And this can be a great asset; invaluable even! But it can also be the worst enemy of your long-term goals.

Susie may have been a great bookkeeper for your $650k a year business; can she grow with you into being the CFO of a $25,000,000 conglomerate that you're trying to build? Chuck may have been the best sales guy for your single location; is he going to cut it for the triple digit locations you're planning?

I'm not suggesting that no long-term employee can grow with your business at the rate you want it to grow. And I'm not suggesting that if they can't, you need to fire them immediately. Not necessarily, anyway.

But it could mean having the dialogue with them that no one likes to have: "I am hiring someone to be your boss." Susie may retain her job as bookkeeper (or perhaps not), but it doesn't mean that she becomes CFO de facto because of her seniority in the company.

And likewise, just because Chuck's been a great salesman doesn't make him a killer sales manager—and there's a lot of historical evidence in a lot of businesses to show quite the opposite.

Keep Chuck rocking as a salesman, and hire a sales manager who will help hire a team that will quadruple sales. Susie's role as bookkeeper will allow the CFO to focus on forecasting, reporting, and tax strategies.

The key point is hiring — and retaining — the right staff to grow with your business. Your rate of success relies on the bodies in the seats; if you have the wrong people in the seat or have the right people in the wrong seat, your business growth can struggle and possibly completely fail to come to pass.

Especially when your business is rocking and rolling, you may find yourself kicking back a little, not making those hard decisions, and perhaps taking your eye off the future. Metaphorically, you've taken your foot off the gas pedal because it seems like the car is self-driving. But when you've developed and cultivated your long-term perspective that has specified goals for your business, it's time to be making those hard decisions so you can realize the growth of which you dream.

Charles "Cork" Walgreen III faced a serious challenge when he became president of the company his grandfather had founded at the young age of 34.

The company was not meeting its profitability goals or its growth targets. It was struggling with its identity. It was a good company, but it had not yet achieved the greatness that Jim Collins would later bestow upon it.

Cork put it like this, "We thought we could sell everything… suits, hammocks, carpets. We were trying to please all people with all types of merchandise that didn't belong in a drugstore."

In addition to their pharmacies, Walgreens had started a number of varied businesses, including a chain of freestanding restaurants, laboratories, manufacturing plants for private label products, and interests in grocer and department store chains.

Cork determined that it was time to get back to Walgreens core business: pharmacy. With that, he initiated a turnaround for the company that many deem unprecedented. Not only did he divest of peripheral businesses, he began a lasting focus on pharmacy services, customer convenience, and investing wisely back into the business.

He also changed the company's view of profitability, switching focus from profit per store to profit per customer visit. He also embraced innovative technology so quickly that his competitors were lost in the dust, leaving the iconic red W a landmark on nearly every corner of the country.

Cork was also hailed as an unrivaled industry leader who advocated the high value of his company's team members and credited his management team and employees with the company's successes, not his own strategies and vision.

When he retired in January 1998,[9] the company had enjoyed 23 consecutive years of record sales and earnings growth under his leadership, had six stock splits and had grown to more than 2,400 stores (from 561 in 1971) generating $13 billion in sales (from $817 million). Over the next 20 years, these sales numbers would dramatically skyrocket even further, as would their profit margin.

Do you think Cork ruffled feathers? You can bet he did. Did he have long-term vision? Yes. Did he cultivate his ego? No. And he made the right hiring decisions to put his business on the path to long-realized success.

Though there is no longer a Walgreen family connection in the leadership of the company, the impact of Cork Walgreen's exceptional leadership cannot be ignored.

Cork was known to follow his grandfather's advice on hiring. Charles Walgreen Sr. was posthumously inducted into the Labor Hall of Fame, and called "a visionary who advanced the causes of working men and women." Secretary of Labor Elaine Chao noted

9   https://news.walgreens.com/press-center/news/charles-r-walgreen-iii-former-walgreen-co-chairman-and-ceo-dies-at-age-80.htm

that by combining his business acumen with professionalism and a positive work environment for employees, Walgreen Sr. was able to create a company that truly cared for its workers. "The company's turnover rate, then and now, remains among the lowest in the retail sector."

How does it start? With good hiring practices. First, I believe in being direct, blunt, and forthright. Honesty up front eliminates confusion and a lot of frustration for both parties. For example, I am as clear as I can be about the role, my expectations, and my requirements for this employment to be a success for both the candidate and the business.

Once they enter the relationship of employee, the last thing I want is for them to be shocked—and I don't want to be shocked either to learn that they had no idea "this" is what they would be doing.

As directly as possible, I explain that the number one thing is that if it is good for the business, it is good for us all. We serve the business, and the business in turn takes care of us. If it is bad for the business, it will be bad for all of us.

Second, if we look at success as being individualized instead of collective, we will none of us be successful. If you're making life better for yourself, you aren't going to be making the business successful. If you're making life easier for your coworkers and your clients, then you're going to be a winner. If all we do is help ourselves, we won't be great; but if ten people around us will be better off because of our actions and engagement with them, then we are going to be that much more successful as we serve our one purpose: the success of the business.

Third, open and honest communication. Tell me if you see something going sideways. I'll do the same. It doesn't matter if it's personal, professional, something in the business or with a client. Keep the dialogue constant, honest, and it will be the most effective. Open feedback both ways is vital to a good working environment.

And last, I tell every candidate that there is an unwritten contract when an employee starts to work for me: Your job is to support the business and me, and my job is to support you and the business. The unwritten contract is that we have each other's backs, and we support each other and the business equally with passion and confidence.

With these blunt and direct approaches to interviewing candidates, I very rarely have the opportunity to see the "first week fail" or the "six month fizzle," because I've been clear and up front about my expectations, my requirements, my commitments, and what I expect in return. It's much better to spend a few minutes in an interview weeding out the candidate who won't respond to the stipulations than to gloss through and sugarcoat it, and have to fire them and rehire and retrain someone else later down the road.

Let's talk about the other side of the coin: firing. I'm equally direct when I have to let someone go, and not once have I regretted letting someone go because I have known every time that I was open, honest, direct, and the business demanded they be cut loose to succeed somewhere else.

If you're facing a situation where you know there's someone who needs to receive less-than-positive feedback, but you haven't had the conversation with them yet, do it now. Be open and honest with them. "My job is your success. But you're not realizing success right now. What do we need to do to get you successful so that I'm also successful?"

If you deliver the message honestly, you'll often get one of two reactions: one, they have no idea what you're talking about, and you have the opportunity to start the dialogue on what you need them to adjust to be more successful. Or they'll delve into all the reasons they already know are the reasons they're not achieving success. Either way, this open and honest conversation is often the start of improvement … or the beneficial exit.

One of my clients told me about a hiring manager they once worked with who pointed out that if someone is not working out for your business, and they need to go, you're actually doing them a disservice by keeping them on staff. In an attempt to "keep them on," you're keeping them out of the job market a little bit longer. You're keeping them from being able to go somewhere where they can be successful.

Ultimately, we want our employees to be like family. We want to have emotional connections to them. But the check on our emotions is our loyalty to the business.

CHAPTER SEVENTEEN

MONEY, STARRING IN THE GOOD, THE BAD, AND THE UGLY

Finance is the art and science of watching money flowing in and out of your business and deciding how to allocate it and determining whether what you're doing is producing the results you want. Accounting is the process of ensuring the data you use to make your financial decisions is complete, accurate, and timely.

Money is deceiving. It is the ultimate distraction. Marriages crumble as a result of its management. Family members become estranged, friends part ways, and it — and the lack of it — result in the downfall of many businesses.

Money can give a false sense of security. Many business owners see money in the bank account and think they're fine, perhaps they can take their foot off the gas pedal. They see money coming in from sales and think we're good, I can relax! They might kick the can down the road and save those hard decisions for another day.

Conversely, you may also see money leaving the account and have no idea where it's gone, but know that it isn't good that it is gone. Where is all the profit going? By nature, most people don't like to cut expenses or make tough decisions, especially when it comes to money.

Money can be difficult because a lack of it means altering the way you do things. It could mean having to do more or do less. It may mean changing focus from what you enjoy doing to what you least enjoy doing. Money can be painful. Many of us also do not have a healthy view of money, either wanting it too much so that we struggle with greed, or not having enough of it which makes us make bad decisions out of fear.

A lot of business owners and entrepreneurs get into a jam financially when they accept bad money from predatory financiers. Namely, the kind of payday loan, merchant cash advances, or "high-risk lending" companies that deliver quick money short-term but draw long-term payments at high percentages back...eating away the profits of a business to nothing.

When you get that quick infusion of cash from a bad lender, you inevitably get less than you anticipated. After "processing fees," you'll also find payments start nearly immediately — sometimes the same day. What started out as $150,000 is whittled down to

$130,000 very quickly, with a $200,000 payback over 9 months. Holy Shitake, Batman!

So get better loans! Easy to say, but if you're like most business owners and entrepreneurs looking for capital, you'll find lenders giving a variety of excuses as to why they cannot lend you significant funds. They don't work with your industry. They need 12 months of financials and your business is only 5 months old. Ownership changes. Your credit score is too low. You have no liquid assets.

One client had every traditional bank loan application turned down because they were solely an online business. With an extensive email list that subscribed to online content that delivered ad revenue from each eyeball on the platform, but no brick-and-mortar building or inventory, they were told there was no viability for a loan despite solid financials and the ability to exponentially grow. There's no end to what can be done in that industry if you have writers, readers, and a platform. But it didn't matter to the banks.

Another client waited over nine months for a "nearly guaranteed" SBA loan to be approved, only to be denied at the last minute due to the regulated industry with which they operated. In the meantime, they had taken a short-term loan that ballooned at 12 months, costing them the ownership of the building they used as collateral.

The temptation for the optimistic and visionary entrepreneur is to look for money in all the right and wrong places. Pursuing viable lending is expensive in time, and it takes effort in an area you likely don't love to spend extra time poring over.

But when you're thinking about money, you have to become an accountant in your mind. Yes, even if you struggled through every math class you ever went through in school. You have to understand the ROI of every dollar that goes out, and the net profit of every sale that comes in. You have to weigh interest rates against payback time frames. You have to have an excessive understanding of what this money can be for you: the good, the bad, and the ugly.

Every successful business must bring in a certain amount of money to keep going. This is a statement many will say "duh" to, but it's also one statement that not every business owner knows to be absolute, concrete, unwavering truth.

There are fundamental decisions that have to be made when you're the leader of a business, and most of them revolve around money. Not having enough cash will shut down a business, and having a lot of revenue but not sufficient revenue to sustain the business and its growth will, too. Business is not about what you make, but what you keep.

You have to understand that because the numbers don't lie, you have to listen to the numbers. Numbers don't lie, but salespeople do, and so do predatory lenders.

Check the numbers you're given, and check them again. Don't just look at the percentage rates or the amount of time it will take to repay, but at the amount they'll take from your cashflow every week, every month. Salespeople are trained to make the numbers sound better than they actually are, so do your own math and split down the payments against your actual numbers, not just your projections.

Can your business survive if the payment is putting your account in the negative every week? Can your business survive if the revenue is sufficient but the payments are eating such a large percentage of your profit margin there is no room for any curve balls or economy shifts or personal challenges?

Evaluate your options and conduct a thorough cost-benefit analysis. Google's famous cafeteria, daycare, dry cleaning, and other fringe employee benefits is a great example of what seems to be a huge cost, but actually repays the company many times over by keeping employees on campus the majority of their waking hours.

Likewise, you must understand that if you're going to send 20% of your net profits to repay a short-term loan for inventory, you'll not be able to put that 20% towards attracting new customers to purchase that inventory.

Paying back $50,000 over a year and paying back $30,000 over six months can be a huge difference to a business's cashflow.

Every decision you make concerning money has to be made from an accountant's mindset. What is the ROI? What is the cost-benefit ratio? What is the loss to your profit margins? How long until you have to make your first payment? Are there personal guarantees? Can your business handle the payments?

And when one bad loan is taken, it can become so difficult to bear the burden that many will stack a second, even a third position until they're literally in business simply to satisfy the debt they've taken. Now you have to have those difficult conversations and decisions that you should have had months ago, and there's nothing left in the account day to day to keep the lights on.

What is the bottom line? The numbers don't lie. And what else is there to do besides lower costs or obtain lending? Here it is. Increase revenue. Sounds simple, right?

It is simple, and that's one thing you're going to have to creatively think out of the box on. How do you make more revenue, realize more profit? What decisions do you have to make in your business to widen the gap between what goes out and what comes in so that you're keeping more than you did last year?

We tend to overcomplicate things, get inside our own heads, and make out like we're doing everything we can already. But are you?

CHAPTER EIGHTEEN

THE BUSINESS IS THE BOSS

For years, I've toyed with the realization that "the business is our master." I realize these days that kind of phraseology isn't considered "PC," but I truly want you to understand that the business is king, master, boss, commander. You, as its owner and leader, are the overseer, the regent, the second in command, the captain. Everything else falls into servanthood to that master/king/boss/soldier.

Whatever metaphor you want to choose for your own internal and external conversations, you get the idea. You aren't the one demanding these hard decisions based on the financials, it's the business. It's not you letting someone go because you're about to not be able to pay them — or perhaps they're not growing with the business at the rate the business demands.

Whatever the conversation is that you must have with your vendors, your staff, your spouse, or yourself: the business is the master. The king. The boss. The Commander-in-Chief. You serve the business.

True, you may be the business owner, and yes, the business takes care of you — if you take care of it. And yes, it can be a benevolent dictator, but it does often serve as a dictator because as we have made very clear in pages prior: the numbers don't lie.

Some have told me this concept actually provides them with some personal relief. Instead of having to be "the bad guy," which entrepreneurs rarely enjoy being, the business is the faceless jerk making the hard decisions that need to be made in order to survive another day, week, or year. Not everyone has a board of directors to "blame" tough calls on. It can be truly heart-wrenching to call your team into the room and tell them you've got to cut payroll by 50% one way or another or the business will fail in a month.

When you're faced with three paths and you're not sure which one to take, you take the one that serves the business. When you're determining if a plan of action is viable, you put it to the test: what serves the business? When you're deciding whether you can give large company bonuses or employee raises or whether to move into that larger space that costs a little more than you hoped, what serves the business?

Too many business owners think they're the boss, or perhaps their spouse is the ultimate boss. We could add a chapter on how important a good marriage is to having a healthy business. Oftentimes emotion leads the decisions instead of facts like the numbers.

Some might even say the customer/client is the boss, and to some degree this may be correct — after all you won't have a business without customers/clients paying for your goods and services.

But when overhead and payroll need to be cut, don't leave these hard decisions and conversations to the end as the last resort when they should have been day one actions. Why? Because when you've put the boss hat on your own head and not allowed the business to dictate from its financials what must happen to ensure its survival, you will ultimately suffer and so will the business.

"I really care about Susie, I can't let her go," or perhaps "Chuck, are we good, I really want to make sure we're on the same page."

These are emotion-based decisions that put you in the boss seat, not the business. The business says you can't afford to pay Susie to be the bookkeeper for a $250k business because you need a CFO for your multi-million-dollar company. Chuck has been meeting quotas but not expanding the impact of your company in the surrounding area.

We don't work for Susie or Chuck or even you. We work for the business. If Susie or Chuck is holding the business back or the business is having a hard time achieving revenue sufficient enough to pay for their salaries, then the business demands you make the difficult decisions for its survival.

Are you helping the business by keeping Susie or Chuck happy? Or is it time to let them find a new opportunity so the business can succeed?

Think of your business as a third person, as if you answer only to it and serve only at its command. The business is the boss. Weigh all decisions, options, choices, and plans against this statement and I am convinced we will watch your business flourish.

ABOUT THE AUTHOR

After years on Wall Street, Joseph Meuse founded Business GPS in order to use his experience and business acumen to help struggling businesses and business-owners.

With offices in Washington DC and Southern California, Meuse and Business GPS are helping thousands of businesses find relief in a post-Covid world by helping them get out of financial hardship, receive government loans, decrease commercial rental payments, negotiate loans to better terms, and improve cash flow – all on contingency.

Meuse is well cast to this position based on his background and proclivities as a seasoned operator, and as a serial entrepreneur himself.

Having started his first business while attending the prestigious College of William & Mary, Meuse spent the next 30 years starting and building over a dozen successful businesses (both US and China-based) and in the process, has helped thousands of other US (and Asia-based) companies execute on their business plans.

Sectors of experience span financial services, investment banking, accounting and finance, IT, business consulting, and legal services, giving Joe a broad perspective on best business practices and how they can be most effectively transferred across categories.

As a thought leader in operationalizing business transformation, Joseph Meuse has been a regular contributor on TV and radio, including CNN, CNBC, and Fox.